How to Get the *Most* Out of the Eucharist

How to Get the *Most* Out of the Eucharist

Michael Dubruiel

Our Sunday Visitor Publishing Division
Our Sunday Visitor, Inc.
Huntington, Indiana 46750

Copyright © 2005 by Our Sunday Visitor Publishing Division, Our Sunday Visitor, Inc. Published 2005

10 09 08 07 06 05   1 2 3 4 5 6 7 8 9

Our Sunday Visitor Publishing Division
Our Sunday Visitor, Inc.
200 Noll Plaza
Huntington, IN 46750

ISBN: 1-59276-139-9 (Inventory No. T190)
LCCN: 2004117796

Cover design by Tyler Ottinger
Cover art, "Lifted Up," by Carol Elder Napoli, courtesy of the author
Interior design by Laura Blost

PRINTED IN THE UNITED STATES OF AMERICA

To my son Joseph,
who has helped me to find in the Eucharist
that which satisfies all that I hunger for in life.

*When all the land of Egypt was famished, the people cried to
Pharaoh for bread; and Pharaoh said to all the Egyptians, "Go
to Joseph; what he says to you, do."*

GENESIS 41:55

CONTENTS

✼ ✼ ✼

*Place upon the altar of your devotion all that you enjoy, all
that you are capable of doing, the whole of the life you live, all
that you hope for; and then offer yourselves as a sacrifice to
God, which is greater than all holocausts.*

—ST. PETER DAMIAN

GETTING THE MOST OUT OF THE EUCHARIST

When you celebrate Mass, consider the sacrifice you are offering.

— St. Charles Borromeo

I have had the opportunity to speak about the Eucharist to people in almost every part of the United States since the release of *The How-To Book of the Mass*, which I wrote several years ago. No matter where I have happened to be, I have received the same response: a dissatisfaction of sorts, often rooted in how things were being done in the local parish.

Some of these people (and an alarming number of young Catholics) longed for the "old" days of the Tridentine liturgy. Yet I know from conversations that I've had with older priests that the old liturgy was subject to many of the same problems as today's Mass.

What *was* different forty years ago was the attitude that Catholics brought to the Eucharist. It was more sacrificial. A phrase one often heard older Catholics use when things didn't go as expected or wished was "to offer it up." This sacrificial attitude guided a generation of Catholics to focus not on themselves but on what God wanted of them.

THE EUCHARISTIC BANQUET

By the time I attended a Catholic college in the early 1980s, those who still had this attitude were ridiculed. I remember a very pious student one day suggesting to another student who was complaining about the difficulty of an upcoming test that he "offer up" the suffering he was undergoing for the poor souls in purgatory. His fellow student replied, "Are you nuts?" Everyone at the table laughed. It was symbolic of a change in the Catholic psyche.

The Holy Sacrifice of the Mass had become the Eucharistic banquet. A picnic table replaced the stone altar in the college chapel, and it was moved from the remote sanctuary at the front of the chapel to the center, in the midst of the congregation. After many years of viewing the Eucharist primarily as a sacrifice, many Catholics now emphasized the meal aspect of the Mass. Fellowship was stressed, and worship seemed to take a backseat.

Pope John Paul II, in his Encyclical on the Eucharist *Ecclesia de Eucharistia*, has mentioned that one of the modern "shadows" or problems with the way Catholics understand the Eucharist is that "Stripped of its sacrificial meaning, it is celebrated as if it were simply a fraternal banquet."[1]

In answer to the Pope's teaching my college chapel has been renovated yet again. The picnic table is gone, replaced by a very ornate altar that is located in the middle of the congregation. Images once removed and stored in closets have returned, and there is now a sense that both God and humans occupy this worship space.

Yet the shadows remain. It is my belief that this downplaying of the sacrificial nature of the Eucharist is the main reason that many of us are not getting the most out of the Eucharist. Over time we lose sight of why we go to Mass or, worse, the Eucharist is relegated to a mere social obligation, one that can easily be skipped.

THE EUCHARIST AS A SACRIFICE

The solution to this modern dilemma is simple — put Jesus back at the center of the Eucharist and you immediately change all of this. In his encyclical Pope John Paul II says, "In giving his sacrifice to the Church, Christ has also made his own the spiritual sacrifice of the Church, which is called to offer herself in union with the sacrifice of Christ. This is the teaching of the Second Vatican Council concerning all the faithful: 'Taking part in the Eucharistic Sacrifice, which is the source and summit of the whole Christian life, they offer the divine victim to God, and offer themselves along with it.' "[2]

As we participate in the Eucharist, not only do we participate in Christ's sacrifice on Calvary but we are called to share in that sacrifice. Just knowing this should change how we view everything that irks us at Mass. Are you:

- Suffering mental anguish — like a crown of thorns is upon your head?
- Weighed down by worldly concerns — like the weight of the cross is on you?
- Feeling powerless — like you are nailed to a cross?

If we take away a sacrificial attitude toward the Eucharist, we are likely to fail to see the connection between our lives and what we do at Mass. We are apt to sit in judgment, waiting to be entertained (whether we are conservative or liberal, what we want to see differs but the attitude is the same). When we fail to bring a sacrificial attitude to the Eucharist, our participation seems at times to be modeled more after Herod's banquet, where Simone's dance cost the Baptist his head, than after the Last Supper of Our Lord, where there was every indication that partaking in this banquet was likely to cost the disciples their own lives. (Indeed, ten of the twelve were martyred, Judas took his own life, and John survived being boiled alive in a cauldron of oil.)

When was the last time that you celebrated the Eucharist with the thought that you were being asked to "offer yourself" — to give your very life? Chances are, you haven't thought of it, but you may have experienced it …

- By thinking "I could be doing something else."
- By asking "Why am I here?"

Yet you weren't doing anything else and you were there — what was missing was the free offering of "your sacrifice," the choice to offer your suffering along with that of the Passion of Our Lord.

Participation in the Eucharist requires that we die to ourselves and live in Christ. If we want to get the most out of the Eucharist, then sacrifice is the key. This is what has been lost on many of us, and if we want to reclaim all the spiritual riches that are available to us we must relearn what it means not only to "offer it up" but indeed to offer ourselves up.

A NOTE OF CAUTION

Now, I want to be clear that what I am proposing in this book is not the "victim-ism" that was sometimes prevalent in the older spirituality of "offering it up." In every situation we are free to choose how we will respond to an event: we can blame someone else for what is happening, or we can feel powerless and do nothing. It is my contention that neither of these responses is Christlike. The experience of "offering up" our lives to God needs to be a positive and co-redemptive act. Thankfully, with God's help we are all capable of freely choosing to respond in this fashion.

Those who promoted the spirituality of "offering it up" in a previous age often quoted St. Paul's words to the Colossians: "Now I rejoice in my sufferings for your sake, and in my flesh I complete what is lacking in Christ's afflictions for the sake of his body, that is, the church" (Colossians 1:24). In offering our sacrifice at the Eucharist, in the same way that we offer up any suffering we endure in life, we take whatever is negative and turn it into a positive, life-giving force both in our own lives and in the lives of those around us. We make up for what is "lacking" for the sake of "his body," the Church — that is, ourselves in communion with all Christians with all of our imperfections and all of our failings. "The miracle of the church assembly lies in that it is not the 'sum' of the sinful and unworthy people who comprise it, but the body of Christ," Father Alexander Schmemann remarked.[3] This is the power of the cross of Jesus Christ, taking what appears to be weakness and allowing God to transform it into strength!

OFFERING OUR S.A.C.R.I.F.I.C.E. AT THE EUCHARIST

Over the past four years I have given a series of talks on this topic. I found it helpful to come up with an easy-to-remember mnemonic device based on the word *sacrifice*. Each letter of S.A.C.R.I.F.I.C.E. stands for an action or attitude that, if fostered, will help us to get the most out of the Eucharist. The nine letters stand for:

> S... Serve
> A... Adore
> C... Confess
> R... Respond
> I... Incline
> F... Fast
> I... Invite
> C... Commune
> E... Evangelize

These actions and attitudes correspond specifically to certain parts of the Liturgy but they are also applicable to how we live out our Christian life. They offer a plan by which we can live out a spirituality of the Eucharist.

The following chapters illustrate how each of the actions and attitudes listed here can be applied to the celebration of the Eucharist. At the end of each chapter there are five additional helps:

1. **Keep Your Focus on Jesus** offers a way to reflect on the action or attitude being discussed in the life and ministry of Jesus.
2. **Learn from the Blessed Virgin Mary** offers Our Lady as a guide for getting the most from the Eucharist. Mary is the perfect Christian and looking to her is the perfect way to learn how to follow her son Jesus. Pope John Paul II has said, "If we wish to rediscover in all its richness the profound relationship between the Church and the Eucharist, we cannot neglect Mary, Mother and model of the Church. . . . Mary can guide us towards this most holy sacrament, because she herself has a profound relationship with it."[4]
3. **Attitude to Foster** offers a simple verse taken from Scripture to help internalize the attitude or action.
4. **Developing a Eucharistic Spirituality** offers suggestions for putting the action or attitude into practice in our daily lives.
5. **A Prayer for Today** offers a prayer to recite or practice to help internalize the action or attitude.

There are also other suggestions throughout the book drawn from the teachings of the Catholic Church. The method being proposed here is simple: We must let go of our judgmental attitude and replace it with a sacrificial attitude. This is so simple, in fact, that in each section I have included a lesson I have learned about putting this into practice from my three-year-old son, Joseph. You'll find that when you approach the Eucharist with the attitude that you have a sacrifice to offer, there will be no end of things to offer God at every Eucharistic celebration!

WHY DO IT?

I was giving a talk at a Catholic parish in rural Ohio a few years ago about the topic of this book. When I had concluded my presentation someone asked, "Why do people care so little about their faith today?"

I told them of a man, a non-Catholic, I had known who cared little about his faith but attended Mass every week with his Catholic wife because he wanted to make her happy. He did this for years, to the point that several priests tried to convince him that he should convert to the Catholic faith since he had been attending the Eucharist for so many years. He refused.

Then he was diagnosed with bone cancer. His condition deteriorated rapidly. In a few months he went from being robust and strong to bedridden and totally dependent upon others. He called for a priest, who heard his first confession and then offered the Eucharist at his bedside, where he received his First Holy Communion. In the last months of his life, his Catholic faith was all that mattered to him.

This led a woman in the group to recall an incident when a tornado had wiped out her family's farm and the family had sat huddled together in the storm cellar, praying the Rosary. At that moment their faith had mattered more than anything else in the world to them.

Someone else mentioned that in the weeks following the 9/11 terrorist attacks on this country he had noticed more people in the Church and more fervency in the way people seemed to pray.

Our faith is a matter of life and death and our faith is totally centered on Jesus Christ. The Scriptures reveal that Jesus did not leave us as orphans but founded a Church. He made the very human apostle Peter the first leader of this Church. He left a memorial of his saving death in the Eucharist and commanded his disciples to perform it.

Getting the most out of the Eucharist is an urgent task, then, because our very life depends upon Christ, and Jesus comes to us in the celebration of his passion, death, and resurrection at every Eucharist. Jesus said that he is the vine and that we are the branches. In the Eucharist we receive the very life that connects us to Christ the Vine.

Jesus told a parable about what happens when a storm comes that lashes out against our very lives (see Matthew 7:24–27). He said that the wise person builds his house (his life) on solid ground, on rock (the image that he used to speak about his church and Peter). The foolish person builds on sand and is destroyed by the storms of life.

The work of building the foundation on which our lives depend takes place every time we participate in the Eucharist. While I was putting the finishing touches on this book I traveled to Florida, right after Hurricane Frances had made a direct hit near Stuart, Florida. I had been scheduled to give a talk in nearby Palm Beach Gardens two days after the storm had hit. The talk was canceled because the church, St. Patrick's, was without power, but I had the opportunity to meet with the pastor of the parish, Father Brian Flanagan, and some of the parish staff. In the midst of much devastation what remains vivid in my mind is how peaceful everyone there was. I know Father Brian to be a man whose deep faith is rooted in the Eucharist, and what I experienced in those days immediately following Hurricane Frances was a literal exposition of Jesus's parable — the storm had come, but because the lives of the people I met were built on solid rock, they were not destroyed.

Isn't this what we all want, a joy that the world cannot take away, no matter what might happen? Our Lord offers it to us at every Eucharist. It is my hope that this small book will help you to better experience this joy, and to discover the richness the Lord's Eucharistic presence can add to your life.

S ERVE THE LORD

S...	*Serve*
A...	*Adore*
C...	*Confess*
R...	*Respond*
I...	*Incline*
F...	*Fast*
I...	*Invite*
C...	*Commune*
E...	*Evangelize*

"You shall worship the Lord your God and him only shall you serve."

MATTHEW 4:10

In my home parish, St. John the Baptist in Fort Wayne, Indiana, the words *Parate Viam Domini* are inscribed over the front doors. The two years of Latin that I had in college and my knowledge of Scripture are enough for me to figure out that the message greeting me each Sunday are the words of St. John the Baptist in the desert, "Prepare the way of the Lord." It is an excellent message to set the tone for the mystery that is about to be celebrated.

PREPARATION

I remember how differently I approached the Mass when as a young man I began to serve at the Eucharist as an altar boy. Before I could serve for the first time, I had to attend training sessions so that I knew what gestures and movements I was to make, and had to study the Latin responses so that I could answer the prayers of the priest at the appropriate time. Sometimes school was sacrificed so that I could serve a funeral mass, or a Saturday afternoon so that the priest could be attended to as he witnessed the marriage vows of a couple celebrating the Sacrament of Matrimony.

The thought and preparation that went into serving at the Eucharist required a sacrifice on my part but kept me focused on why I was there. Adults who serve as lectors, ushers, extraordinary ministers of the Eucharist, and choir members often mention feeling similar sentiments when they first take on these acts of service. Yet with time we are all apt to find ourselves going through the motions without much preparation and indeed without much thought about the fact that we are serving God in our respective roles at the Eucharist, and this inattentiveness is to our detriment. Making preparations is the work of a servant, and in the celebration of the Eucharist it is the work of every disciple of Christ.

THE WAY

"The Way" is one of the oldest names for the first followers of Christ. Jesus often told his disciples that he came to show them "the Way" to the Father, that God's ways were not our ways, and that He was the Way. The routine that we can fall into at the Eucharist happens precisely when we stop seeing what is taking place as "different" from everything else that we experience in life. Not only is it different, but if we truly enter into the Eucharist with a spirit of sacrifice, it will change the way that we view everything in our lives. The tension between Christian beliefs and the beliefs of "the world" is understood only when we come to embrace "the way" of Our Lord Jesus Christ.

Most converts to Christianity have a clear sense of the saving power of Jesus as "the Way." Faithful, lifelong Catholics may not have as keen an understanding until they experience the difference their faith has made to them in contrast to the rejection of that faith in one of their children. Yet understanding that "the way" of Christ is not business as usual can keep us from thinking that we have nothing to prepare for when we celebrate the Eucharist. Once we realize that God's ways are not our ways, we will always see the need to "prepare ourselves for these Sacred Mysteries" we are about to celebrate.

LIVING THE EUCHARIST

Throughout the day, when the events of the day do not go your "way," before frustration has a chance to set in, stop and ask yourself what God's way might be for what the day has given you. Try to think of a similar incident in the life of Christ to the one in which you find yourself — how did Our Lord handle the situation?

THE LORD

Jesus told his followers that when they had done all that had been commanded of them they should say: "We are unworthy servants; we have only done what was our duty" (Luke 17:10).

Our lives often are like a field of weeds with pressing concerns that can seem to take priority, but indeed the weeds are not as powerful as they might seem, and remembering who is Lord, Master, and God can help us put everything into perspective.

LESSONS LEARNED FROM A THREE-YEAR-OLD

Anyone who has a young child has a built-in reminder that coming to the Eucharist requires servitude. Preparations have to be made so that the child will be taken care of during the celebration. Sometimes this means making sure that a child's prayer or Mass book is in his or her possession. At other times it simply means having tissue for a runny nose or having an extra dose of patience to deal with any outburst that might occur. One thing is certain: any parent who has a young child is already bringing the attitude of a servant to the Eucharist. If I get a little too comfortable in the pew and lean back in the posture of a spectator, my three-year-old will pretty quickly remind me that I'm not there to relax but to serve.

> *"Whoever receives this child in my name receives me, and whoever receives me receives him who sent me; for he who is least among you all is the one who is great."*
>
> — LUKE 9:48

Having a young child in our midst, whether it is our own or someone else's in the next pew, is a great reminder to us to humble ourselves, that in serving the child we may serve the Lord himself.

OUR *S*ACRIFICE

MAKE AN OFFERING OF YOURSELF.

We give up the desire to be in charge and adopt an attitude of service.

WHOSE WAY ARE WE PREPARING?

Every Sunday when I come to the Eucharist and am confronted by the words inscribed in stone over the entrance of my parish church, "Prepare the way of the Lord," I am reminded that the first sacrifice I must make at this Mass is my own ego, and as I strive to relinquish the need to be in control of what will happen at this Eucharist I ask, "What does my lord bid his servant?" (Joshua 5:14).

We all face the same struggle. Some of you may protest:

- "The ushers don't make me feel welcome in my church."
- "My parish priest preaches too long."
- "The musicians in our church are out of control."
- "People are too loud and talk too much before the Eucharist."
- "The people dress too well or too poorly."

Each of us, if given the opportunity to share what we think is keeping us from getting the most out of the Eucharist, is apt to come up with our own list. Recently I asked this question online and received a deluge of responses. Many were true abuses of the liturgy, and were worthy of being reported to the diocesan bishop, but just as many were not.

When I shared my amazement at the number of responses with my wife, she very keenly mused, "They all feel helpless, like they have no control." As soon as she said this I realized that this was exactly the same thing I had heard from priests and musicians, the two groups who are most often the target of the congregation's ire. Priests who come into a new parish and encounter established ways of doing things with which they do not agree and yet are powerless (at least at first) to change and musicians who are hired to provide a parish with beautiful music yet find themselves restrained by parish staff or established practice to playing pieces they feel are less than worthy of the liturgy often express frustration at their lack of control.

This brings home a point that we do not like to admit: None of us is in control, no matter what our function is in the liturgy. Yet we are all tempted to think that if we were in charge we could make it all perfect.

The greatest suffering that I've endured at any celebration of the Eucharist has been the few cases where someone, whether it was the presider, a musician, or, as in several cases, a member of the congregation, thought he or she could make the liturgy more perfect by his or her own inventions. Here are some examples of this type of behavior, all of which actually happened:

- An Easter Sunday where a visiting priest tried to woo the congregation by creating a "Mass" of his own making, never once using the words prescribed by the Church from beginning to end.
- A musician who saw himself as in a battle with the celebrant and who continually and loudly played music over the presider's attempts to pray the prescribed prayers of the Church.
- A congregant who screamed out for the priest to stop because "no one" —meaning herself— "knew where he was" in the liturgy.
- A congregant who held up a crucifix as he processed toward the altar to receive the Eucharist and then, after receiving the Eucharist, turned and exorcised the congregation with loud prayers and wild gesticulations of the cross.

Now, you may think of some of these people as being mentally ill, and perhaps some of them were, yet a case could be made that when any of us "lords" it over another we are a little off in the head, especially if we are doing so and claiming to be a follower of Jesus. None of this is new, of course; even in Jesus's time there were those who sought to take control and lord it over others. Yet Jesus addressed this issue directly, and clearly specified the subservient attitude that would be required of his followers:

Jesus called them to him and said, "You know that the rulers of the Gentiles lord it over them, and their great men exercise authority over them. It shall not be so among you; but whoever would be great among you must be your servant, and whoever would be first among you must be your slave; even as the Son of man came not be served but to serve, and to give his life as ransom for many."

— MATTHEW 20:25–28

GETTING THE MOST OUT OF THE EUCHARIST

If you want to get the most out of the Eucharist you have to check your "I" at the door. The "I" that wants things, that endlessly critiques the way things are done, and that demands things be done in exactly a certain way (meaning "my way," not God's way). I think it was Peter Kreeft who once said that the famous song, "I Did It My Way," sung by such great artists as Frank Sinatra and Elvis, is the national anthem of hell. The way of the world may be to do things "our way" but the way of Christ is to do things his Way. We therefore consciously have to leave "my way" at the door and in exchange take up an attitude that asks "how may we be of service to you, Lord, in this celebration of the Eucharist?"

THE INSTITUTION OF THE EUCHARIST BY JESUS

On Holy Thursday, the day on which the Church celebrates the institution of the Holy Eucharist, the gospel reading for the Mass does not mention Jesus taking bread and wine but rather an act of service that Jesus performed at the Last Supper. The Lord taking bread and wine and declaring it his body and blood is mentioned in the Second Reading for that Mass, but not in the gospel.

The gospel for Holy Thursday is from John's gospel. It is the story of Jesus rising from the table and shocking his disciples by doing something totally unexpected, washing their feet.

Peter refuses to have his feet washed at first but acquiesces when Jesus tells him that it is necessary if Peter is to have any inheritance in him.

If you are like me, you can relate to Peter. There is something in Peter's character that perfectly illustrates what we all are like in our fallen nature. We are proud. We want to be in control. We like Jesus, and we want to be part of his crowd, but we also want to tell him what to do.

"Do You Know What I Have Done for You?"

When Jesus had finished washing the feet of his disciples, he rose and resumed his place at the table and asked them a simple question: "Do you know what I have done for you?"

There are several ways to take this question which Jesus posed to us, his followers; let me suggest two.

What Jesus Has Saved Us From

The first possible meaning relates to what Jesus has done for us by his sacrificial act on the cross: Do we know what Jesus has saved us from?

You may know enough to say, "Jesus has redeemed us from the bondage of original sin," but unless you know what the lived consequences of this sin are, you cannot fully appreciate what Jesus has saved you from. The Catechism of the Catholic Church spells out the nature and effects of original sin in paragraphs 397–412. Here I briefly summarize this teaching and contrast it with how Jesus has reversed the "curse" of original sin.

First, in the sin:

- Man "let his trust in his Creator die in his heart and, abusing his freedom, disobeyed God's command" (CCC 397).
  — *Jesus trusted in God completely, even to death on the Cross, praying in the Garden of Gethsemane, "not my will, but thine, be done" (Luke 22:42).*
- Man "*preferred* himself to God," thereby turning his back on the Creator (CCC 398).
  — *Jesus, though he was the form of God, did not deem equality with God; rather, Jesus lowered himself, taking the role of a servant (see Philippians 2:6–7).*

As a result of original sin:

- People are "afraid of the God of whom they have conceived a distorted image" (CCC 399).

— At the Conception of Jesus, his Mother was told: "Do not be afraid, Mary, for you have found favor with God" (Luke 1:30).
— Jesus told his followers, "I will warn you whom to fear: fear him who, after he has killed, has power to cast into hell; yes, I tell you, fear him! Are not five sparrows sold for two pennies? And not one of them is forgotten by God. Why, even the hairs of your head are all numbered. Fear not; you are of more value than many sparrows" (Luke 12:5–7).

- The original "harmony in which they [Adam and Eve] found themselves … is now destroyed" (CCC 400).

— Jesus set the example of reversing this disharmony, so that St. Paul would pray, "May the God of steadfastness and encouragement grant you to live in such harmony with one another, in accord with Christ Jesus" (Romans 15:5).

- "The control of the soul's spiritual faculties over the body is shattered" (CCC 400).

— Jesus's death and our incorporation into it at baptism restore the right order, as St. Paul wrote to the Romans, "Let not sin therefore reign in your mortal bodies, to make you obey their passions. Do not yield your members to sin as instruments of wickedness, but yield yourselves to God as men who have been brought from death to life, and your members to God as instruments of righteousness. For sin will have no dominion over you, since you are not under the law but under grace" (Romans 6:12–14).

- "The union of man and woman becomes subject to tensions, their relations henceforth marked by lust and domination" (CCC 400).

— Jesus said, "Have you not read that he who made them from the beginning made them male and female, and said, 'For this reason a man shall leave his father and mother and be joined to his wife, and the two shall become one flesh?' So they are no longer two but one flesh. What therefore God has joined together, let not man put asunder" (Matthew 19:4–6).

> — *St. Paul instructed the followers of Christ that "the wife does not rule over her own body, but the husband does; likewise the husband does not rule over his own body, but the wife does" (1 Corinthians 7:4) and in an often misquoted passage he told the Christian husband to love his wife "as Christ loved the church and gave himself up for her" (Ephesians 5:25).*

- "Harmony with creation is broken: visible creation has become alien and hostile to man" (CCC 400).

  > — *Jesus commanded nature and nature obeyed, both in healing the sick and calming the storm. He told his disciples, "In my name ... they will pick up serpents, and if they drink any deadly thing, it will not hurt them; they will lay their hands on the sick, and they will recover" (Mark 16:17–18).*

- "Death makes its entrance into human history" (CCC 400).

  > — *Jesus raised the dead and was raised from the dead, and promised eternal life to anyone who believed in him, proclaiming himself to be "the bread which came down from heaven, not such as the fathers ate and died; he who eats this bread will live forever" (John 6:58).*

Knowing what Jesus has done for us will give us a greater appreciation of the Bread of Life that we receive when we approach his altar at every Eucharistic celebration. It is literally a matter of our life or our death!

LIVING THE EUCHARIST

Is your Christian life dominated by the fallen worldview? Do you strive with the help of the Holy Spirit and the nourishment of the Eucharist to live the new life of the kingdom that Jesus offers?

The Sacrificial Meal That Jesus Has Given Us

A second possible meaning to the question Jesus asked relates to the Lord's Supper that He had just given to his disciples. Jesus had taken bread that he said was his body and wine that he said was his blood and given it to his disciples. Then he got up from the meal and washed his disciples' feet — lowering himself, doing the task of a servant, then returning to his place. Some Scripture commentators point out that symbolically this action of Jesus mirrors his incarnation, God lowering himself to become one of us, and then after his death and resurrection, ascending back to the heavens. Yet Jesus did not abandon his apostles. He promised to send his Spirit and commanded them to celebrate the memorial of his Passion, death, and resurrection — the Eucharist.

Do we know what Jesus has done for us in giving of himself to us when we celebrate the Eucharist?

If you have ever attended the ordination of a priest, it is likely that you have been struck by various parts of the ritual. The prostration and the laying on of hands are both deeply moving, but the one part of the ordination rite that has struck me every time I have witnessed it is the moment when the newly ordained priest kneels before the ordaining bishop, who hands a chalice and paten to the priest as he says to the newly ordained: "Accept from the holy people of God the gifts to be offered to him. *Know what you are doing, imitate the mystery that you celebrate: model your life on the mystery of the cross.*"[5]

In that brief exhortation there is an excellent message for every one of us: "know what you are doing, imitate the mystery that you celebrate: model your life on the mystery of the cross." It echoes Jesus's question to his disciples, "Do you know what I have done for you?"

St. Paul spells out what Jesus has done for us in his Letter to the Philippians 2:5–7: "though he was in the form of God, [Jesus] did not count equality with God a thing to be grasped, but emptied himself, taking the form of a servant, being born in the likeness of men." Jesus is the Son of God who lowered himself and became one of us.

The God who is above everything we can think of, who is the very reason that we live and the reason that the universe exists, humbled himself to become a part of creation. This is in direct opposition to fallen humanity that sought "to become like God" when it disobeyed God's command in the Garden of Eden.

Our desire to be in control is part of our fallen nature. Many of us live with an illusion that we are in control. We are taught to plan for every eventuality, to insure ourselves for every possible disaster, but if we do not realize that only God is in control, we are living in a fantasy world. Think of the parable that Jesus told of the rich man (see Luke 12:16–21) who built bigger barns to store his large harvest; he was foolish, Jesus said, because he was to die that night. His material wealth could not save or help him once he was in the grave. The rich man thought he was in control of his destiny but, like every one of us, found out that he was not — God was and is.

Jesus rescues us from the chaos that life is without him. Pope John Paul II has said, "In the Eucharist our God has shown love in the extreme, overturning all those criteria of power which too often govern human relations and radically affirming the criterion of service: 'If anyone would be first, he must be last of all and servant of all' (Mk 9:35). It is not by chance that the Gospel of John contains no account of the institution of the Eucharist, but instead relates the 'washing of the feet' (cf. Jn 13:1–20): by bending down to wash the feet of his disciples, Jesus explains the meaning of the Eucharist unequivocally."[6]

"I HAVE GIVEN YOU AN EXAMPLE"

Jesus told his disciples that he had given them a model to follow. He said, "If you know these things, blessed are you if you do them" (John 13: 17).

The traditional tale of the fall of Satan is that it was due to his refusal to serve: *non serviam*, "I will not serve," was the devil's reply to God. Inflated by pride, he would not obey. Fallen humanity shares this trait, as Jeremiah the prophet says: "For long ago you broke your yoke and burst your bonds; and you said, 'I will not serve'" (Jeremiah 2:20).

In opposition to Satan and fallen humanity is Jesus Christ. Jesus did not come to be served but to serve. We who follow him are "in Christ" and we are to imitate him at the liturgy. If we want to get the most out of the Eucharist we need to start by fostering the attitude of Christ the Servant.

COUCH POTATO CATHOLICS?

It strikes me that at the heart of every problem we experience in the Eucharist today is a fundamental stance of someone who will not serve but wants to be the one served — sort of a couch potato Catholic.

St. Benedict, in his Rule, explains the proper attitude the follower of Christ is to have at prayer: "If we do not venture to approach men who are in power, except with humility and reverence, when we wish to ask a favor, how much must we beseech the Lord God of all things with all humility and purity of devotion? And let us be assured that it is not in many words, but in the purity of heart and tears of compunction that we are heard."[7]

If someone very important were coming to your house, you would want to make sure that the person was at ease, you would look after his or her comfort, and that person would be the center of your attention until his or her departure. Likewise, if we truly serve God at our celebration of the Eucharist, God will be our focus. Our hearts and minds will be raised to him.

If your role is to preside at the liturgy, you must serve the liturgy faithfully

> *Behold, as the eyes of servants*
> *   look to the hand of their master,*
> *as the eyes of a maid*
> *   to the hand of her mistress,*
> *so our eyes look to the LORD our God,*
> *   till he have mercy upon us.*
>
> — PSALM 123:2

as the Church has handed it down to you. If you are a musician, the music must serve the liturgy, helping all to raise their voices as one to God. If you function as a lector you must proclaim the readings with great care so that all may hear the Word clearly. Every person in the congregation has a role to serve in the Eucharist.

FOSTERING AN ATTITUDE OF SERVICE

If you have ever held a position in a service industry then you know that one of the principal ways of fostering an attitude of service is by presuming that the customer is always right. Having been in that position myself in many different jobs over the course of my life, I know that many times the customer isn't right, but I also know that when you treat them as if they are they are more apt to come to the truth than when you treat them in an arrogant manner.

HELP FROM THE FATHERS OF THE CHURCH

Let your prayer, then, be no mere pronouncing of words with the lips. Devote your whole attention to it, enter into the retreat of your heart, penetrate its recesses as deeply as possible. May he whom you seek to please not find you negligent. May he see that you pray with your whole heart, so that he will deign to hear you when you pray with your whole heart.

— ST. AMBROSE

Fostering an attitude of service toward God in the Eucharist is not exactly the same thing as assuming that the customer is always right, however, because unlike the human customer, who may in fact be wrong, God *is* always right! Believing that can lead us to some rather startling conclusions, when we come to Mass and with every moment of our lives. A great illustration of this attitude of service is found in the Second Book of Samuel when King David flees Jerusalem after it has been taken over by his son Absalom. As

David flees, a kinsman of King Saul named Shimei comes out as the king passes by and begins cursing him, continually throwing stones at David and his servants. One of David's servants, Abishai, says to David, "Why should this dead dog curse my lord the king? Let me go over and take off his head" (2 Samuel 16:9).

King David's response is to rebuke Abishai and to wonder "If he is cursing because the LORD has said to him, 'Curse David,' who then shall say, 'Why have you done so?'" (2 Samuel 16:10). They travel on and Shimei continues to follow them, cursing while throwing stones and dust.

What if this were our attitude? What if we were to take a second look when something happens that isn't in our plan, perhaps even to think that the person cursing us might be doing so because God is telling him or her to do so?

A servant is always ready to serve. This is a sacrifice that Christ demands of his followers, and one that when we embrace it will help us to get the most from the Eucharist we celebrate.

FURTHER HELPS

1. Keep Your Focus on Jesus

Whenever you desire to "control" what happens in the Eucharist, or suffer because you sense someone else is hijacking the liturgy,

- Think of Jesus washing the feet of his disciples.
- Think of Jesus telling his followers to take up their cross and follow him.
- Think of Jesus saying that he did not come to be served but to serve.

Keeping your focus on Christ will prevent the devil in his attempts to distract you from the purpose of the Eucharist.

2. Learn from the Blessed Virgin Mary

Following the example of the Blessed Virgin Mary we declare ourselves at God's service. "Behold, I am the handmaid of the Lord" (Luke 1:38) was Mary's response to the Angel Gabriel's announcement that God would become incarnate within her. When we come to the Eucharist, God desires to continue the incarnation within us, and Mary teaches us how we should approach so great a gift.

Mary's reaction to the angel's message gives a supreme example of the sacrifice we can bring to every celebration of the Eucharist. When confronted with anything that does not go according to our plans, we need to open ourselves up to what God might be asking of us.

3. Foster an Attitude of Service

When Joshua realized that he was being confronted by a messenger of God, someone who at first he was not sure was a friend, he asked, "What does my Lord bid his servant" (Joshua 5:14)?

When we have the right stance toward God in our worship this is the question we will ask when confronted by anything that disturbs us: "What does my Lord bid his servant"?

4. Developing a Eucharistic Spirituality

Empowered by Christ, we should seek to serve God and anyone God places in our path throughout the day. "How may I serve you?" should be the question ever on our lips, whether at home, at work, or in recreation. We can find concrete ways to serve Christ in the many guises in which he comes to us in the poor and the weak.

5. A Prayer for Today

These beautiful words of St. Augustine, taken from his Soliloquies, may help you to ask God for the grace to offer yourself, so to be at his service:

O God, at last You alone do I love, You alone I follow, You alone I seek, You alone am I prepared to serve, for You alone by right are Ruler, under your rule do I desire to be. Direct, I pray, and command whatever You will, but heal and open my ears, that I may hear Your utterances. Heal and open my eyes, that I may behold Your signs. Drive delusion from me, that I may recognize You. Tell me where I must go, to behold You, and I hope that I shall do all things that You command. O Lord, most merciful Father, receive, I pray, Your fugitive; enough already, surely, have I been punished, long enough have I served Your enemies, whom You have under Your feet, long enough have I been a sport of falsehood. Receive me fleeing from these, Your house-born servant, for did not these receive me, though another Master's, when I was fleeing from You? To You I feel I must return: I knock; may Thy door be opened to me; teach me the way to You. Nothing else have I than the will: nothing else do I know than that fleeting and falling things are to be spurned, fixed and everlasting things to be sought. This I do, Father, because this alone I know, but from what place to approach You I do not know. Instruct me, show me, give me all that I need for the journey. If it is by faith that those find You, who take refuge with You then grant faith: if by virtue, virtue: if by knowledge, knowledge. Fill me with faith, hope, and charity. O goodness, singular and most to be admired![8]

ADORE GOD WITH PRAISE AND THANKSGIVING

S...	Serve
A...	**Adore**
C...	Confess
R...	Respond
I...	Incline
F...	Fast
I...	Invite
C...	Commune
E...	Evangelize

The *Baltimore Catechism* was used as a primary teaching tool when I was a child. Even though I probably was taught with it for only the first three

> *O come, let us worship and bow down,*
> *Let us kneel before the Lord,*
> *our Maker!*
>
> — PSALM 95:6

or four years of my Catholic education, like others before me I haven't forgotten the simple lessons it taught me, like:

Q. Who is God?
A. God is the Creator of heaven and earth, and of all things.

"All things" includes me and everyone else on the earth, along with everything else that I can perceive. God is the maker of all that is, and as such is the most important Being that exists. My very existence depends upon God.

It follows then, and this is from the modern Catechism of the Catholic Church, that "to adore God is to acknowledge, in respect and absolute submission, the 'nothingness of the creature' who would not exist but for God. To adore God is to praise and exalt him and to humble oneself" (CCC 2097).

WHEN YOUR MIND WANDERS

One of the most frequent complaints that people who genuinely want to get more out of the Eucharist raise is that they find that their mind wanders at Mass. The cause of their distraction may be as simple a question as "Did I turn off the car lights?" or as weighty a concern as "I wonder how I'm going to pay the mortgage or rent this month?" It is understandable, given the hectic pace of life, that when we try to quiet ourselves in the presence of God we often find that our minds are cluttered with many distracting thoughts.

HELP FROM THE FATHERS OF THE CHURCH

For often in the very sacrifice of praise urgent thoughts press themselves upon us, that they should have force to carry off or pollute what we are sacrificing in ourselves to God with weeping eyes. Whence when Abraham at sunset was offering up the sacrifice, he was troubled by birds of prey sweeping down on the carcasses, but he diligently drove them off, so that they might not carry off the sacrifice being offered up (cf. Gen. 15:11). So let us, when we offer a holocaust to God upon the altar of our hearts, keep it from birds of

> *prey that the evil spirits and bad thoughts may not seize upon that which our mind hopes it is offering up to God to a good end.*
>
> — ST. GREGORY THE GREAT

When Jesus came to visit the two sisters of Lazarus, the sister named Mary sat at Jesus's feet and listened to him while the other sister, Martha, feverously worked in the kitchen to entertain their houseguest. Finally Martha came to Jesus and complained about the fact that Mary wasn't helping her. Wandering minds, worriers, and a host of others don't like what Jesus told Martha: "Martha, Martha, you are anxious and troubled about many things; one thing is needful. Mary has chosen the good portion, which shall not be taken away from her" (Luke 10:41–42).

I was discussing the topic of this book with a priest and he told me that in his many years of presiding at the Eucharist in churches around the world he thought that the organist was the most distracted member of almost every parish, "always fiddling with the music for the next piece, kind of a visual mind wandering." It is easy to be caught up in worrying about doing a good job to the point that we forget why we are doing the job. Jesus tells the Martha in all of us, "One thing is needful."

When we come to the Eucharist, are we adoring God, or worshipping something else?

OUR SACRIFICE

MAKE AN OFFERING OF ANY FALSE GODS.

We give up anything that we think is more important than God.

GOD ALONE

Over the entrance to the cloister of the Abbey of Gethsemane in Kentucky are two simple words that are not simple at all in practice: God Alone. What really is necessary? God. What truly is worth worrying about? Our relationship with God.

Jesus said, "One thing is needful."

If you want to get the most out of the Eucharist, adore God! Worship the One who can save you from whatever life may bring, even death!

A COMMANDMENT

In 1989 something happened to me that I still think a lot about. I had come into our parish church in order to obtain the Blessed Sacrament to bring to the sick in the local hospital. As I approached the sanctuary of the church, I knelt down to spend a few minutes of prayer before setting out. It was then that something compelled me to prostrate myself on that spot on the carpeted floor. This was something I had seldom done before. So there I knelt with my hands and head pressed to the floor.

I felt something rough pressing into my forehead. Raising my head from the floor and feeling my forehead, I found pieces of the Eucharist (this parish used homemade unleavened bread at their Sunday Masses, a type of bread that crumbled quite easily). Feeling around the floor, I found more pieces of the Eucharist there. I picked them up and placed them into the pyx that I was carrying with me and took them to the pastor of the parish. The pastor immediately put a stop to the parish using the homemade bread until they could find a way to keep this "abuse" of the Blessed Sacrament from occurring.

This incident is noteworthy to me because of the "impulse" that came over me to adore those unseen pieces of the Blessed Sacrament on the floor.

In Scripture this impulse to adore happens whenever someone comes into contact with a messenger of God, with an event that reminds them of God, or with God himself in the person of Jesus. Abraham does this in Genesis 18:2, Balaam does it in Numbers 22:31, Joshua does it in Joshua 5:14, the blind man does it to Jesus in John 9:38, and the disciples do it to Jesus in Matthew 28:9. Those tempted to adore God's works, however, are condemned in Scripture.

When John falls down to worship an angel in the Book of Revelation, the angel scolds him, "You must not do that! I am a fellow servant with you and your brethren who hold the testimony of Jesus. Worship God" (Revelation 19:10). Likewise, when Cornelius bows down to worship Peter, he is told by the apostle, "Stand up; I too am a man" (Acts 10:26), and when Paul and Barnabas are the recipients of unwanted worship they tear their garments and beg the people to recognize that God alone is to be worshipped (see Acts 14).

The point is that God alone is to be adored. If you want to get the most out of the Eucharist you need to worship the Lord! The first three commandments given to Moses emphasized the necessity of worshiping God alone.

1. I am the Lord your God: you shall not have strange Gods before me.
2. You shall not take the name of the Lord your God in vain.
3. Remember to keep holy the Lord's Day.

This means that we must not worship false Gods. What are some of the false gods that can present themselves as "goods" at the Eucharist? They are the same today as they would have been for those who experienced Christ in the flesh:

1. Ideology: Liberal or Conservative

In Jesus's time the Sadducees and the Pharisees held rival ideologies of how best to be a worshipper of God. Yet when God showed up in their midst in the person of Jesus, neither group could accept him — Jesus didn't fit their image of God.

In our own time good and well-meaning people fall into the same temptation, one that masks itself as a good but is really a sin of pride. There are people who accept what the Holy Father teaches on some issues but reject what he says on others based not on whether it matches the truth of the gospels but rather on whether it matches their ideology or what they wish God was like.

When it comes to the worship of God, we must insure that it is God that we adore and not our own idea of who God is or should be.

2. Looking for a Human Savior

Jesus is our savior. If we are looking for a priest, a parish community, the perfect worship space, or excellent music — though all of these are good things — we risk making an idol out of these things and missing God, who is omnipresent. The effectiveness of the Eucharistic liturgy depends upon God, not us. Reverencing Jesus — no matter how bad the preaching, music, church building, or anything else that might be our personal pet peeve — puts our focus where it belongs. Those who tried to worship the apostles were scolded that this was not where their focus should be, but rather on God. Ministers both clerical and lay need to remember this: none of us is the savior; only Jesus holds that title.

GETTING THE MOST OUT OF THE EUCHARIST BY ADORING GOD

From a positive standpoint, then, what can we do to adore God in the Eucharist?

First we must foster a sense of reverence for God. The actions in the Mass of kneeling, bowing, and beating our breasts all have meaning. They cause us to consciously call to mind that God is present and to focus all of our attention on what God wants of us at the present moment.

Second, we need to worship the Eucharist outside of Mass in order to foster a deeper communion with our Eucharistic Lord when we receive his awesome gift at Mass. When we actively worship Our Lord Jesus Christ in the Blessed Sacrament we grow in awareness of what it means to receive him at Communion. Pope John Paul II has written about this as a necessary element to restoring an awe of the precious gift of the Eucharist. A Franciscan friend recently told me that when preaching about the Eucharist to young people, he begins by telling them to "Be amazed," paraphrasing the Holy Father's injunction.

Coming aside to reverence Christ in the Eucharist, realizing that he is before us, has the same power to change us as he did to those who came into his earthly presence.

LIVING THE EUCHARIST

Try to find time to make a visit to a chapel or church to adore the Lord in the Blessed Sacrament. Give Christ whatever time you have, whether a little or a lot. Make acts of worship in his presence.

Consciously call to mind God's presence throughout the day, no matter where you are.

Third, we need to understand what the Catechism of the Catholic Church calls "the implications of faith in one God." It means:

- "Living in thanksgiving" (CCC 224).
- "Trusting God in every circumstance" (CCC 227).

LESSONS LEARNED FROM A THREE-YEAR-OLD

My son Joseph walked into the room while I was putting together the material for this chapter. When he walked in I was having a difficult time coming up with a good illustration for what "living in thanksgiving" means in the concrete and I wasn't thankful that he was bothering me. Then it struck me that the point of living in thanksgiving is simply that what I might otherwise perceive as an interruption becomes an intervention, once I adore God above all things.

God had sent Joseph into my room. This hit me when I sent him away and he said "Thank you," as he went off. For a period of his young life he had the habit of saying "thank you," not after he had been given something that he was appreciative of but rather when he had been told to do something, I think he thought that "thank you" meant "okay." Yet this is exactly what living in thanksgiving is, saying "thank you" to whatever God presents to us in the daily events of our lives.

"LIVING IN THANKSGIVING"

Living in thanksgiving literally means always having gratitude on your lips.

The late great Orthodox liturgist Alexander Schmemann felt that the meaning of "thanksgiving" — the literal translation of the Greek word *Eucharist* — had been lost on modern people. We tend to limit giving thanks to only those things that we receive that we perceive as good. Yet Schmemann argues that for the early church "giving thanks" was something the Christian did because the Kingdom of God had been restored in Jesus Christ.

Our very inclusion in Christ is reason enough to give thanks; the fact that God has spoken to us in the Word is another reason to give thanks; the fact that Christ has saved us and shares his Body and Blood with us is another reason to give thanks; and the fact that Christ has given us a mission is yet another reason to give him thanks! In fact, you will recognize that at the point in the celebration of the Eucharist that each of these things is mentioned, we express our thanks, either as a congregation, when we say, "Thanks be to God," or through the presider, when he says to God, "We give you thanks."

Because of what Christ has done for us we now have a vantage point in life that those who do not know Christ do not have. The liturgy is a mystery of light, and we are on the mountaintop of the Transfiguration and know that Jesus rises from the dead — that he is victorious over our enemies. Therefore, as St. Paul tells the Thessalonians, we can "Give thanks in all circumstances; for this is the will of God in Christ Jesus for you" (1 Thessalonians 5:18).

> ## LIVING THE EUCHARIST
> *Practice giving thanks to God at all times. Make it a habit to step back when you judge something negatively and to ask God to help you to see it in his will.*

"TRUSTING IN GOD IN ALL CIRCUMSTANCES"

When Our Lord spoke about his Second Coming, an event that every celebration of the Eucharist looks forward to and prays for in a joyful manner, he laid out the signs that will precede that coming, and indeed they are all rather horrible — that is, if all your hope is invested in your 401K. Yet notice the contrast between the unbeliever and the believer:

> And there will be signs in sun and moon and stars, and upon the earth distress of nations in perplexity at the roaring of the sea and the waves, *men fainting with fear and with foreboding of what is coming on the world*; for the powers of the heavens will be shaken. And then they will see the Son of man coming in a cloud with power and great glory. *Now when these things begin to take place, look up and raise your heads, because your redemption is drawing near.*
>
> — LUKE 21:25–28 (EMPHASIS ADDED)

While one crowd is dying of fear because everything seems to be crumbling around them the other crowd, the believers, stand up and look to the heavens. Why?

If we truly place our faith in God, we will trust in him no matter what happens. In fact, the way that we see will be completely different. Jesus referred to unbelievers as blind and believers as those who truly see. Seeing that God is the "one thing needful" keeps us from putting our trust in anything else.

St. Benedict, in his Rule, counsels those who want to follow Christ "to prefer nothing to the love of Christ."[9] This means that we must love Christ above everything else, and that being loved by Christ must be our first priority in life.

BEING LOVED BY JESUS

In Mark 10:21 in the account of the rich young man, Mark tells us that Jesus, "looking upon him loved him, and said to him, 'You lack one thing; go, sell what you have, and give to the poor, and you will have treasure in heaven; and come, follow me.' "

Notice that because Christ loves the rich young man, he points out what the young man lacks. It is out of love that Jesus tells him to get rid of all his possessions.

Christ's love will reveal similar deficiencies in us. Our Lord looks upon us and recognizes what we really need. However, we often come to him with our own ideas about what we need.

If we prefer our own ideas to the love of Christ, we too will join the rich young man who walks away sad, "for his possessions were many." We may possess the world, but without Christ it is nothing!

LOVING JESUS

In John 8:42, Jesus is engaged in a heated argument with those who oppose him. He says to them, "If God were your Father, you would love me, for I proceeded and came forth from God; I came not of my own accord, but he sent me." We know, therefore, that Jesus is God, and we should prefer nothing to God and his love, which Jesus has revealed to us perfectly.

How do we know if we truly love Our Lord? He addresses this in John 14:23-24: "If a man loves me, he will keep my word, and my Father will love him, and we will come to him and make our home with him. He who does not love me does not keep my words; and the word which you hear is not mine but the Father's who sent me." We love Our Lord by doing what he commands us to do.

ADORING GOD WITH PRAISE AND THANKSGIVING

One of my favorite quotes is from the journals of Father Alexander Schmemann: "God, when creating the world, did not solve problems or pose them. He created what He could call 'very good.' God created the world, but the devil transformed the world and man and life into a 'problem.' "[10] If we want to adore God with praise and thanksgiving we are going to have to learn to stop seeing everything as a "problem" or "interruption" and begin to be open to seeing God's goodness and interventions even in the most unlikely of places.

Many of the most horrific sins ever committed by human beings happen because people see problems where they should see blessings. If we do not adore God above all, we risk doing horrible things as we serve whatever else we have put in God's place.

HELP FROM THE FATHERS OF THE CHURCH

Human beings are created for the purpose of praising God. The Lord demands nothing else in the same manner that he requires praise and thanksgiving of us. For that reason he made rational beings and distinguished us from animals by our power of speech so that we might praise and glorify him continually.

— ST. JOHN CHRYSOSTOM

PROBLEMS VERSUS BLESSINGS

A prayer that is recited by those who pray the Liturgy of the Hours on every major feast day of the Church is an example of the kind of thanksgiving that should be the prayer of all believers. It is called the *Benedicite*, after the many times that the word "Bless" is used in it. In this case "Bless" is another way of saying "give thanks and praise." The setting is found in the book of Daniel, where three young men are placed in a fiery furnace, something I'm sure even the most faithful among us would be tempted to think of as a "big problem." As they enter the fiery furnace to what would seem like a certain death, one of them, Azariah, prays:

> Blessed art thou, O Lord, God of our fathers, and worthy of praise; and thy name is glorified for ever. For thou art just in all that thou hast done to us, and all thy works are true and thy ways right, and all thy judgments are truth. Thou hast executed true judgments in all that thou hast brought upon us and upon Jerusalem, the holy city of our fathers, for in truth and justice thou hast brought all this upon us because of our sins. For we have sinfully and lawlessly departed from thee, and have sinned in all things and have not obeyed thy commandments; we have not observed them or done them, as thou hast commanded us that it might go well with us.
>
> —DANIEL 3:3–7

It is a prayer of thanksgiving, sounding very much like a Eucharistic Prayer that is prayed at the Mass we attend. Those trying to exterminate the three men, hearing the prayer, stoke up the flames, and the three pray a prayer that includes the following:

> Bless the Lord, fire and heat, sing praise to him and highly exalt him for ever. Bless the Lord, winter cold and summer heat, sing praise to him and highly exalt him for ever. Bless the Lord, dews and snows, sing praise to him and highly exalt him for ever. Bless the Lord, nights and days, sing praise to him and highly exalt him for ever. Bless the Lord, light and darkness, sing praise to him and highly exalt him for ever. Bless the Lord, ice and cold, sing praise to him and highly exalt him for ever. Bless the Lord, frosts and snows, sing praise to him and highly exalt him for ever. Bless the Lord, lightnings and clouds, sing praise to him and highly exalt him for ever. Let the

earth bless the Lord; let it sing praise to him and highly
exalt him for ever."

—DANIEL 3:44–52

There has been many a winter morning when I was scraping
snow and ice from my car when the words of this prayer have
come to my lips, often, I must confess, rather sarcastically.

Too often we forget that God has a plan that doesn't quite
match up to ours. If our plans and possessions dominate us, we
can become very ungrateful in life and perhaps even feel cursed.
Yet if we die to ourselves and adore God, giving thanks to God
in all things, even when we are standing in the flames, or freez-
ing in the ice and snow, we'll find that God has a reason and purpose for everything. As St. Teresa of Ávila said, "There is no such
thing as bad weather. All weather is good because it is God's."

THANK GOD AHEAD OF TIME

There is an American friar whose cause for sainthood is currently
before Rome. His name is Father Solanus Casey; he was a
Capuchin Friar who ministered in Detroit, New York, and Huntington, Indiana. He died over forty years ago. I often walk the
grounds of the former friary where he served in Huntington and
think about his ministry. Born of Irish immigrants, he was sent
to German seminaries where the priests taught him in German
how to speak Latin. He didn't fare too well — who would?

Eventually he was ordained but not allowed to preach doctri-
nal sermons or hear confessions. In a time when there was more
of a caste system in religious life he was given a "brothers' job" as
porter. People sought him out near and far. They found great wisdom in his words, and great miracles of healing were recorded
after his prayer and touch. Many were converted.

In many ways, it would seem that he would have had much to
be bitter about. He was obviously one of the most gifted friars in
the community, but he was treated as one who had little to offer.

Yet he was not bitter, and his advice to people who requested prayer and healing is interesting. He told them to "thank God ahead of time" — as an act of faith. He often also had them enroll in a Mass association as a way of giving thanks to God.

This is a beautiful message for us: to thank God in all things, to be thankful for everything that life brings to us even if to all appearances it doesn't seem there is anything to be thankful for, and to thank God ahead of time, trusting that in God's time good will come from it all.

The Eucharist is all about "giving thanks," and how much you and I can do so at any given moment is dependent upon how deeply we are adoring and worshiping God. Offering God our sacrifice of praise and thanksgiving will help us to get the most from the Eucharist.

FURTHER HELPS

1. Keep Your Focus on Jesus

When Satan tempted Jesus in the desert, Our Lord rebuked the devil saying, "Begone, Satan! For it is written, 'You shall worship the Lord your God and him only shall you serve'" (Matthew 4:10).

When you are tempted to worship anything else, no matter how lofty it might seem, call to mind this incident from Our Lord's life.

2. Learn from the Blessed Virgin Mary

When the Blessed Virgin Mary was called "Blessed among women" by her cousin Elisabeth she responded with "My soul magnifies the Lord, and my spirit rejoices in God my Savior," (Luke 1:46–47). She pointed to God and worshiped only him.

Following Mary's example, we should seek to "decrease" in order that God may "increase" as we adore him above all.

3. Foster an Attitude of Adoration

St. Paul told the Thessalonians to "Rejoice always, pray constantly, give thanks in all circumstances; for this is the will of God in Christ Jesus for you" (1 Thessalonians 5:16–18). When we foster this attitude our hearts will be focused on adoring God at every moment of our lives.

4. Developing a Eucharistic Spirituality

A concrete way to prefer the love of Christ throughout the day when faced with countless other "loves" is to hear the words Jesus spoke to Peter addressed to yourself: "Do you love me more than these?" (John 21:15).

5. A Prayer for Today

Recite this prayer of St. Teresa of Ávila often:

> *Let nothing trouble you,*
> *let nothing make you afraid.*
> *All things pass away.*
> *God never changes.*
> *Patience obtains everything.*
> *God alone is enough.*

CONFESS YOUR BELIEF IN GOD

S...	*Serve*
A...	*Adore*
***C*...**	***Confess***
R...	*Respond*
I...	*Incline*
F...	*Fast*
I...	*Invite*
C...	*Commune*
E...	*Evangelize*

If you confess with your lips that Jesus is Lord and believe in your heart that God raised him from the dead, you will be saved.

—ROMANS 10:9

One night when a group of believers had gathered to pray in a country where such a gathering was forbidden by law, a cry went out when two soldiers burst through the doors. They yelled out that they would give anyone in the room a chance to leave before

arresting those who refused to do so. A few of the gathered immediately bolted out of the room.

As soon as they left, the soldiers closed the doors and said, "We
are believers too, but we couldn't trust those who were not ready
to be arrested for their faith." Putting down their guns, they joined
the others in prayer.

When you and I hear the word *confess* we are apt to think of
it in terms of our sins, but the word also means to acknowledge
one's belief. The two meanings, when it comes to Christianity, are
very related. What we consider to be sinful has a lot to do with
how much we really believe in God.

People throw their beliefs about God around quite freely these
days, usually prefaced by "Oh, I don't think God cares about that."

Christians believe that Jesus has revealed God and what God
is like to us. Jesus formed a group of disciples around him and
told them that God's spirit would stay with them until the end
of time. This group was to hand down his teaching, baptize
other followers, forgive sins, and teach all that Jesus, the Son of
God, had commanded them to pass on. Peter had a special role
in this group.

Jesus revealed the love of God to us by dying for us and leaving us a memorial of his death in the Eucharist. The word *memorial* had a special meaning for the Jewish people of Jesus's time.
It didn't mean recalling the past, as it does for us today, but rather
it meant making present a past event. Thus, when we come
together at the Eucharist, we are present at Calvary and witness
once again what God is like through Jesus.

People who die for any cause care a lot. Jesus has revealed to
us that God cares a lot! God desires our salvation.

If we want to get the most out of the Eucharist, we need to
confess: We must confess belief in God, as we do in the Creed,
and confess that we are not always the greatest of followers of
Jesus.

OUR SACRIFICE

MAKE AN OFFERING OF YOUR UNBELIEF AND SINS.

We beg God to aid us in all our struggles to be faithful.

One area of spirituality that has been under attack for the past forty years is the "emphasis on sinfulness" that seems to have dominated the spirituality of all religions from the beginning of time. Those who have bought into this removal of sinfulness from their spirituality have found that after awhile God has very little to do with it.

Sin essentially is anything that breaks our relationship with God. Remove sin and you are essentially removing God from the picture — because you are admitting that it really doesn't matter if you are offending God or not. It would be like being in a relationship with your spouse and refusing ever to admit any wrongdoing — one would expect such a relationship to be in grave trouble.

Admitting that we are not living up to our part of the relationship is a healthy part of the struggle to stay in continual communion with God. If we are doing it with "sighs and tears" it means that we are not just doing it out of habit but rather are emotionally feeling what we are saying. St. Ignatius of Loyola would have retreatants pray for the gift of tears when they meditated on their sinfulness, and this is a practice that should be restored.

I remember standing in a confessional line during a Marian pilgrimage that I made in the late 1980s and watching people emerge from the outside confessional stations (the priest sat in a chair, while the penitent knelt beside him, visible to all gathered there) wiping tears away. It was touching, because it gave me the sense that these people weren't just listing off faults but experiencing a heartfelt conversion from a life without God to a life that the penitent truly wanted to live with the help of God. We should all pray for the gift of tears for our failings.

My great-grandfather would always be wiping tears away when he returned from receiving communion. I found this deeply significant as a child, and it is something I've never forgotten. Involving our emotions in our relationship with God is a great grace that we should strive to have in our relationship with him.

Real contrition for our sins involves a firm resolve to involve God in those parts of our lives where we have excluded him in the past. By being aware of God's presence at all times we likely will amend our lives in the future.

LESSONS LEARNED FROM A THREE-YEAR-OLD

When my son admits to disobeying either his mother or me his bottom lip will quiver and he can barely admit to his misdeed. Often as soon as the confession leaves his lips he is on the floor, weeping. It moves us to see how badly it hurts him to have dishonored us.

Isn't this the same way we should feel when we who confess that we believe in God act as though we do not? It is all about love, and perhaps we do not experience the contrition of a three-year-old because our love for God has grown cold. Could it be that because we have committed the same sins for so many years, we have come to define ourselves by them?

I'M NOT OKAY

I once heard Franciscan Father Richard Rohr say that the pop psychology view of the human person is "I'm okay, you're okay" but that the gospel message was "I'm not okay but that's okay with God." St. Paul said, "But God shows his love for us in that while we were yet sinners Christ died for us" (Romans 5:8).

Archbishop Fulton Sheen used to say that "it used to be that only Catholics believed in the Immaculate Conception; now everyone believes that he or she is immaculately conceived." Dr.

Karl Menninger penned a famous book with the title, *Whatever Became of Sin?*

The loss of the sense of personal sin greatly reduces our capacity to feel the necessity of being saved by Christ. We risk having to hit rock bottom before we realize how far we have fallen, if we do not regularly acknowledge our sinfulness and our need to be saved from ourselves.

THE FALLEN WORLD

Previous generations of Christians had a deeper understanding of the fallen nature from which Christ came to save us. When I recently mentioned the fallen nature of humanity in the course of writing another book, the editor queried me as to whether what I was stating was even "Catholic," so foreign has the notion become to the modern follower of Christ.

If we want to get the most out of the Eucharist, we have to understand what Jesus, the Bread of Life, came to save us from, and how he can save us from our sins.

HELP FROM THE FATHERS OF THE CHURCH

If a precious garment is not put away into a box that is soiled, by what line of reasoning is the Eucharist of Christ received into a soul soiled with the stains of sin?

— ST. AUGUSTINE

ADMITTING OUR NEED

There is often talk about the way "modern" Catholics believe, picking and choosing what they believe and bypassing what they don't. It has been termed cafeteria Catholicism — what it is in reality is intellectual sin. We accept Christ's teaching only so far as it agrees with what we already think. When it challenges us, we ignore it.

Jesus didn't accept this from his disciples. When he announced the doctrine of the Eucharist in John 6 many disciples ceased to follow him because they found the teaching too difficult (see John 6:66, notice the numbers). Did Jesus yell out, "Oh, that's okay — take what you like, ignore the rest"? No, instead he turned to those who had not left him and asked, "Do you want to leave me too?"

Our reluctance to accept the Lord's teaching, "in my thoughts and in my words, in what I have done and what I have failed to do," may be our most persistent sin, one that we constantly need to confess openly, as we do at the beginning of every celebration of the Eucharist.

WE ARE ALWAYS SINNERS

One of my favorite prayers is the Jesus Prayer. It is a simple prayer, taken from the Scriptures, one that can be prayed anywhere simply by repeating the words "Lord Jesus Christ, Son of the Living God, have mercy on me, the sinner," over and over slowly. I often pray it throughout the day, whenever I find myself waiting: in the car at a traffic light, in an airport waiting for a flight, in an office waiting for an appointment or at church waiting for the Eucharist to begin.

As I pray this prayer I often imagine that I am one of the blind men spoken of in the gospel who cried out to Jesus as he was passing by.

The Jesus Prayer is essentially an Eastern Christian prayer. Eastern Christians do not have a problem with acknowledging that they are sinners, but I think that Western Christians do.

DIFFERING VIEWS OF SIN

If you are a pre-Vatican II Catholic, chances are you grew up with a fear of sin. You probably never went to Holy Communion unless you went to Confession the night before. You felt "clean" until the next time you sinned (sometimes as soon as you left the church by thinking some uncharitable thought).

After the Vatican Council, some Catholics gave up on sin; they either felt that if God would love us anyway then there was no sense in constantly confessing and then turning around and committing the same sins all over again or they accepted a secular view that did away with calling anything a sin. Both views essentially miss the point. We are sinners and we need God at every moment, and the more we are aware of our sin the more we should be aware of our need for God.

The mistake of the older view of sin was that those who subscribed to it sometimes failed to learn from past failures; the mistake of the newer view is that those who subscribe to it act like nothing is a failure. To truly accept forgiveness and mercy for our sins we have to realize that even though there are times when we need sacramental reconciliation because we really aren't relying on Christ at all, in truth we also need to be reconciled to him at every moment of the day.

Even if our view of our own sin has been somewhat skewed recently, however, our prayers still reflect the faith of the Christian Church that "we are sinners." When I was doing research for *The How-To Book of the Mass* I found that almost all of the commentators complained that there was way too much focus on sin in the Mass. Some even suggested new ways to interpret this age-old obsession.

Recently I was in a parish that had a special song that was sung during Lent for the penitential rite. You know what was strange about this song? It had nothing to do with asking for mercy or forgiveness — the reference to sin had been totally removed from the song. Once again, this was missing the point.

LORD HAVE MERCY ON ME, THE SINNER

Jesus was most associated with sinners during his earthly ministry. He was widely criticized for it. He portrayed as righteous the man who stood in the back of the Temple with head bent, beating his breast and asking the Lord to have mercy on him the sinner —

whereas the unjustified man stood up in the very front, thanking God that he was not like other men.

We are sinners, and bringing a sense of sinfulness to the Eucharist (indeed to all prayer) puts us in the right posture toward God and, I might add, toward each other. A recent Vatican document on the Eucharist says, "a proper examination of conscience helps us to be benevolent towards our neighbors, to share their fragility, and to pardon them."[11] In other words, calling to mind our own sinfulness makes us less judgmental of the sinfulness of others. Is it any wonder, in this modern age when sin is denied, that people are judged so harshly? In previous times people were no less sinful, but they were more often accepted as fellow sinners as all waited in the same confessional line on any given Saturday afternoon.

If the first option for the Penitential Rite is used we begin by publicly confessing that we are sinners both to God and to the people standing around us — and we beseech the people around us (both those we see and those we don't, such as Mary, the angels, and the saints) to pray to God for us. It is a touching prayer, and especially so if we pray it as if our very life depends upon it.

TEACH ME TO PRAY!

One day a boy was watching a holy man pray on the banks of a river in India. When the holy man had completed his prayer the boy went over and asked him, "Will you teach me to pray?" The holy man studied the boy's face carefully. Then he gripped the boy's head in his hands and plunged it forcefully into the water. The boy struggled frantically, trying to free himself in order to breathe. Finally, the holy man released his hold. When the boy was able to breathe, he gasped, "What did you do that for?" The holy man said: "I just gave you your first lesson." "What do you mean?" asked the astonished boy. "Well," said the holy man, "when you long to pray as much as you longed to breathe when your head was under water — only then will I be able to teach you to pray."[12]

Every Mass begins with a chance for us to remember our own plunge into the waters of baptism, and throughout the Mass we recall all that separates us from God, namely our sins and our idols. When the priest or deacon asks us to call to mind our sins, we should do so. We should pay attention to what pops into our heads at that moment. God may reveal to you an area of sinfulness (something that is separating you from perfect communion with him) at that moment. Don't be surprised at what comes up but place it before God at this moment in the Mass so that he can transform it. Recall that God is your Savior, not yourself. Allow God to save you from your sins in his mercy. Believe that God's mercy is greater than your sins.

When Jesus began the celebration of the Last Supper, he began it on a sad note, saying that one of the gathered disciples was about to betray him. Isn't it interesting that all of those gathered asked, "Is it I, Lord?"(Matthew 26:22). In that simple question was a confession both of belief in who Jesus was and of humility and potential sinfulness. Only one asked Jesus, "Is it I, Master?" While Judas acknowledged his humanity, he did not confess belief in Jesus as "Lord," a title that the people used for God in the time of Jesus.

DIVINE MERCY

The encounter with Jesus that takes place in every celebration of the Eucharist calls us to conversion. The more we recognize Jesus in the opening of the Scriptures and the breaking of the bread, the more this becomes apparent. When Jesus first encountered Peter fishing in the Sea of Galilee, the Lord gave Peter some fishing advice. Peter humored the Nazarene and found that the catch of fish was beyond anything that he had ever experienced before. This made him realize that Jesus was unlike anyone that he had ever encountered. So what did Peter do? He made a twofold confession: "Depart from me, for I am a sinful man, O Lord" (Luke 5:8). In recognizing the divinity of Jesus, he also was made aware of his own sinfulness. What did Jesus do? He told him, "Do not be afraid; henceforth you will be catching men" (Luke 5:10). Then Peter followed the Lord.

The journey that Peter set out on that day is similar to the journey that each of us takes after our baptism, and like Peter we may sin again whenever we fail to remember who God is and who we are. Peter was sure that he would be willing to die for Christ even when Jesus told him that he would end up denying him not once but three times. The Lord was right, Peter was wrong. We, too, fall, time and again, after numerous resolutions that we will never sin again. In a matter of seconds we are passing judgment on someone or, even worse, once again falling into sin.

The twofold confession that we make at every Eucharist can change our lives if we speak these words with heartfelt conviction. When we confess our belief in God, we are saying that it is God whom we trust — not our sins and failings, not what others think about us, but God alone.

When Jesus took a Roman coin and asked whose image was engraved upon it, he was told that it was Caesar's. In response to a question about taxes, Jesus told his followers to give to Caesar what was Caesar's (that is, the coins with Caesar's image upon them). We are the coins of God. We bear God's image, and like our earthly coins that bear the inscription "In God We Trust," it is God alone whom we must confess as our Lord.

Most of our acts of conversion are feeble attempts when we turn to God and ask Him to trust in us, but this is not what the spiritual life is about. It is only when we acknowledge our own untrustworthiness and seek instead to put our trust in God that we can experience true communion with God.

Turning to God is what the spiritual life is all about. It begins and ends with an act of trust in God's love and mercy. There is nothing more tragic than when someone ceases to believe that God could ever love him or her — or when someone feels that he or she has committed a sin so great that God could never forgive.

God's love and mercy are always available to those who seek them. Our own despair and the act of closing ourselves off from God's mercy are the only things that can keep us from receiving it.

The devotion to the Divine Mercy that swept the Catholic world in the late 1900s and continues to thrive today is a great way to keep our focus on God's love and mercy by calling to mind the mercy of God each day at 3:00 p.m. The Lord's private revelations to St. Faustina were that his death on the cross was for our sins, and that he lamented the fact that people were not availing themselves of his mercy. The Lord told St. Faustina that she would become his Apostle of Mercy. The simple prayer, "Jesus, I trust in you" is a powerful antidote to the many other voices that seek to destroy our lives. Focusing on the crucifix and meditating on the Passion of Christ as the supreme sign of God's love and mercy are powerful ways to remind ourselves of how much God loves us.

God is our Savior. Jesus, we trust in you!

FURTHER HELPS

1. Keep Your Focus on Jesus

Focusing on the image of Jesus on the cross should remind us of how much God loves each of us and the horrible price of our sins. Think of the words that Jesus spoke from the cross:

- "Father, forgive them; for they know not what they do" (Luke 23:34), a word of forgiveness for our sins.
- "Father, into thy hands I commit my spirit!" (Luke 23:46), a word of trust in God.

2. Learn from the Blessed Virgin Mary

Our Lady was immaculately conceived but still confessed wonderment at the announcement of God's plan to use her, saying in response to the Archangel Gabriel's announcement: "How shall this be, since I have no husband?" Mary's trust was in God and not in her own actions to bring about God's plan for her.

We can follow Mary's example by trusting in God and choosing to obey God at all times, confessing our belief and admitting our failings as we place our trust entirely in God.

3. Foster an Attitude of Trust by Confessing

The story of the man whose child needed Our Lord's healing touch provides us with a perfect model for fostering an attitude of trust. The man told Jesus, "I believe; help my unbelief!" (Mark 9:24).

When we have difficulty believing we must not give into our doubt but rather must turn to God with our unbelief, asking him to help us.

4. Developing a Eucharistic Spirituality

Make an examination of conscience both in the middle of the day and before retiring in the evening. Focus on those areas where God has not been the Lord of your life and on how allowing other things to take importance has kept you from experiencing the new life that God wishes you to have in Christ.

5. A Prayer for Today

Say the Jesus Prayer by repeating the words "Lord Jesus Christ, Son of the Living God, have mercy on me, a sinner," slowly, over and over, throughout the day.

> *Lord Jesus Christ, Son of the Living God, have mercy on me, a sinner.*

RESPOND BY PARTICIPATING

S...	Serve
A...	Adore
C...	Confess
R...	**Respond**
I...	Incline
F...	Fast
I...	Invite
C...	Commune
E...	Evangelize

There was a famous liturgist who wrote beautifully about the Mass in the 1970s. He was in great demand all over the country and spoke quite eloquently about how beneficial the new changes in the liturgy would be if they were implemented in the right way. It so happened that in the town where the liturgist taught there was a Catholic Church that was

> I will thank thee for ever,
> because thou hast done it.
> I will proclaim thy name, for it is good,
> in the presence of the godly.
>
> — PSALM 52:9

noted for being very resistant to change. You might say that they were resistant to any response at all during the Mass. When the presider would greet them with "The Lord be with you," they collectively said nothing. The noted liturgist asked the bishop of the diocese to consider making him the pastor of the parish, and the bishop agreed. The bishop hoped that the professor would be able to transform the life of the parish, making it a model of reform for the rest of the diocese.

Six months later the liturgist was institutionalized, having suffered a nervous breakdown. Even after his recovery he never spoke very convincingly again about the liturgy. I attended Mass at the parish that did him in ten years later. I heard about this incident when I asked a priest in a neighboring parish why the parish was so dead. The lack of response among the worshipers had destroyed the life of that parish church.

On another occasion I attended a weekday Mass in a large parish in upstate New York. There were three people in attendance. When I responded to the priest I felt as though I were shouting, because the other three said nothing. I muted my response but I still heard no response. That evening I attended a Novena to St. Anthony in the same church. The congregation was standing room only. The response to the prayers was thunderous. The faith of the people was infectious.

Recently I attended a weekday celebration of the Eucharist at the cathedral church in Charleston, South Carolina, at 7:00 a.m. There was a good crowd on hand and the way the congregation responded woke me up! They knew how to respond!

All of us have had our experiences, good and bad, of the Mass. Yet how many of us realize our own role in making those experiences what they are?

LESSONS LEARNED FROM A THREE-YEAR-OLD

My son knows only a few responses to the Eucharist. He can make the Sign of the Cross, can give the Sign of Peace, and knows the word "Alleluia." He is quite animated when it comes to the singing of the "Alleluia." This seems always to have the effect of causing those around him, including myself, to be more mindful of how they respond to the Eucharist.

Joseph also insists on putting the envelope into the basket when the offertory is taken up. If there is a Second Collection he'll insist that I fork over some money so that he can put it in. His generosity in giving all that he has to give has renewed my spirit on many a dreary day.

If you want to get the most out of the Eucharist, respond appropriately.

OUR SACRIFICE

MAKE AN OFFERING OF YOUR VOICE AND BODY TO GOD.

We respond with a heartfelt response to Our Lord's gift.

MILITARY EXPERIENCE

You may have heard horror stories (or even experienced them first-hand) from people who have served in the Armed Forces of their experiences in basic training, the initial initiation that turns a civilian into a soldier. I went through basic training at Fort Dix, New Jersey, in 1977. Among the many, many memories I have of those eight weeks of my life are those of having to answer "Present" whenever my name was called off by the drill sergeant. We learned quickly that if we didn't respond with a lot of gusto a drill sergeant's face would be pressed into ours, yelling, as we stood there terrified. It was a great motivation to "respond" appropriately.

A few years later I found myself stationed overseas in Turkey. Every Sunday three or four of us would travel in a military van to attend Mass in Istanbul at the Italian Consulate, some fifty miles from the military base. When I had been in Turkey for six months a tragic event occurred, and one of the soldiers I was stationed with was killed when a terrorist sprayed bullets at a group of our soldiers waiting for the military bus. The base commander warned us not to travel into Istanbul unless it was absolutely necessary.

Sunday came and I watched to see if the van that would take us to Mass was there. It was, and three of the regular Mass-goers got in, and then they waited for me. I waved them off and they left without me. As I stood there it dawned on me that here I was, halfway around the world, ready to die for my country, but I wasn't ready to die for my Lord. On the next Sunday I was on the van that took me to Mass.

THE BODY OF CHRIST

St. Paul said, "For to me to live is Christ, and to die is gain" (Philippians 1:21). Our Lord said that "Unless a grain of wheat falls into the earth and dies, it remains alone; but if it dies, it bears much fruit" (John 12:24). At every Mass we must die to ourselves and allow our hearts to beat as one with the body of Christ, the Church. The Church is the body of Christ collectively. None of us is Christ individually.

If we think of this image of the body of Christ and of all that are present at Mass as members of that body then I think we begin to see that the body should move, speak, and act as a whole. Our actions should be unified, as the Holy Spirit unites us into the body, giving praise in unison with the Son to the Father.

MONK CARRYING A SIGN

I attended Saint Meinrad College in southern Indiana and frequently visit the monastery there. I would say that in all my experiences of how participation in the Mass can be catechized, the lessons I learned there still stand out as exemplary. On our first day at the college we were told when to stand, when to bow and why, and how to sing so as not to be heard.

Visitors to the monastic hours don't often know these lessons, and several times while I've been there a monk has left the choir and carried around a large sign admonishing the visitors to "sing quietly." The goal of monastic prayer sung is that all voices join to become one voice, the voice of Christ, praising God. This is the ideal of everything we do at Eucharist, and I would ask you to imagine the "monk carrying the sign" whenever you are at Mass.

> ### HELP FROM THE FATHERS OF THE CHURCH
> *Our Lord Jesus Christ, the Son of God, prays for us and prays in us, and is prayed to by us. He prays for us as our Priest; he prays in us as our Head; he is prayed to by us as our God.*
>
> —ST. AUGUSTINE

HOW DO WE RESPOND?

Every celebration of the Eucharist provides us with a variety of ways to respond, a variety of ways to offer ourselves to the celebration. Some of these require sacrificing our personal tastes and likes for the good of the whole. Let's look at some concrete ways we respond at the Eucharist:

Singing

Singing is one way that we act in unison and yet it is often the way we may choose to protest our incorporation at Mass. Regardless of whether you like the choice of music or not, sing. Die to yourself — so that Christ may live within you.

As St. Augustine said, *Cantare est bis orare,* "To sing is to pray twice."

Remember the "monk carrying the sign" and sing not to be heard but so that your voice may join with the voices of the rest to become one voice praising God.

Gestures

When I have brought non-Catholic friends to the Eucharist with me the one thing that always gets them is the gestures. To those unfamiliar with the ritual, we Catholics seem to do a lot of moving around during the Mass.

We make the Sign of the Cross when we bless ourselves with holy water upon entering the Church; we beat our breast at the Confiteor; we sign our forehead, lips, and heart in preparation for the gospel; we bow at the mention of the Incarnation in the Creed; we share a Sign of Peace with those around us; we bow before the Eucharistic Lord when we receive him under the forms of bread and wine; and we receive the blessing of the priest at the end of Mass. We also genuflect, stand, sit, and kneel at the appropriate times.

Unfortunately over the past forty years the unison of the body of Christ on this count has suffered. Perhaps we need to all be taught from scratch these gestures that we are supposed to do and when we are supposed to do them at the Eucharist.

These actions should be done in unison with the entire congregation. I suspect that some of us feel uncomfortable with performing some of these signs. I confess to feeling awkward "beating my breast" but I do it anyway, cringing as I make the gesture — it's an opportunity to die to myself in order to live in the body of Christ.

The Mass is not a time to perform gestures that one favors but that are not part of the official rubrics of the Church, nor is it a time to protest when we think that a particular community has adopted a posture that seems wrong to us. Let me be clear here: I'm not talking about personal acts of piety that we do privately but rather public acts — things we do that draw attention to ourselves. The Eucharist is not the time for these public acts; instead it is a time for all of us to act as one.

The story is told that when St. Monica came to Italy to see her son, St. Augustine, she was upset at the way Mass was celebrated in Milan. A certain posture was used in Milan that was not done in the same way in her parish in northern Africa. She complained about it to St. Ambrose, who told her, "When in Rome do as the Romans!" If it was good enough for St. Monica it should be good enough for us — do whatever they do where you are, and remember that you are part of the body of Christ, not Christ himself!

ABUSES OF THE LITURGY

People are very critical of priests and the way they celebrate Mass, but in my experience most priests follow the rubrics very carefully. I wish the same could be said for the rest of us. I have a friend who is fairly pious but refuses to sing. I often quote to him the words of Jesus, "They are like children sitting in the market place and calling to one another, 'We piped to you, and you did not dance; we wailed, and you did not weep'" (Luke 7:32).

There is a very large family I know who attend daily Mass as a family. I'm always impressed with their piety until we get to the Sign of Peace. I've made the mistake of sitting near them a few times. When the priest or deacon says, "Let us offer one another the sign of peace," they stare stoically straight ahead and refuse to acknowledge anyone around them. There is nothing worse than stretching your hand out to the person standing next to you at the Sign of Peace and being ignored.

There are others who insist on performing gestures or postures that are not part of the ritual. Standing when everyone else is kneeling, holding hands (a post–Vatican II favorite) when no one else is doing it during the Our Father, and genuflecting when everyone else is bowing before receiving the Eucharist are all examples of this.

We need to take our role seriously in the body of Christ and act as one as Jesus says, "even as I and the Father are one."

With Our Voices

The rule of singing so that our voices blend as one applies to how we respond vocally too. The first factor to be considered when responding with our voice is that we actually mouth the words. We have parts to say in the Eucharist and we should say them while reflecting on what they mean.

The second concern is that we respond with the congregation, at their pace. I have stood next to people at celebrations of the Eucharist who have raced through the responses, usually loudly, as though God had hired them to coach the rest of us to speed up our part of the Eucharistic sacrifice. Every congregation has its dominant pace, often guided by the presider, and we should follow that pace, not try to set it.

I have occasionally attended the Eucharist at a Trappist monastery where the response is much slower then I and most visitors are used to. When one of the readings in the Mass is completed and the lector says "The Word of the Lord," there is a long silence before the monastic community responds with "Thanks be to God." Again, visitors to the monastery often break the silence with a "Than —" before realizing that no one else is joining them. The slow response of the monks has helped me whenever I have been a part of their Eucharist to reflect more deeply on what I am responding to at the various parts of the liturgy.

On the flip side, some years ago there was a Jesuit priest who traveled throughout the South saying as many as ten Masses on a Sunday, covering hundreds of miles. In order to accomplish this he presided at what could only be termed as a rapid response celebration of the Eucharist. As quickly as the congregation responded, he was on to the next part. I once witnessed a Sunday Mass in a parish with over 1,200 people in attendance that was over in twenty minutes, and this with singing (only one verse of each song) and the addition of a recitation of the Divine Praises after the very short homily for protection against hurricanes and storms.

A third concern is the tone and feeling we use when we respond in the Mass. We should adopt our tone and feeling from the congregation. Our responses should not "single" themselves out. I once knew a woman who was active in the Charismatic movement who would voice her responses loudly and with great emotion. In a congregation made up of like-minded individuals I doubt she would have even been heard but in a congregation where the majority were a little more stoic it was clearly out of place. We offer our voices to the congregation by joining them not by trying to "show" them how they should respond.

By Giving

Another way that we respond at the Eucharist is by practicing stewardship. In Acts 20:35 St. Paul says, "In all things I have shown you that by so toiling one must help the weak, remembering the words of the Lord Jesus, how he said, 'It is more blessed to give than to receive.'"

Pope John Paul II made this phrase of Jesus's the subject of his Lenten Message for 2003. In his message the Holy Father said:

> Believers are called to follow in the footsteps of Jesus Christ, true God and true man, who, in perfect obedience to the will of the Father, emptied himself (cf. Phil 2:6 ff), and humbly gave himself to us in selfless and total love, even unto death on a cross. Calvary eloquently proclaims the message of the Blessed Trinity's love for human beings of all times and places.[13]

Every meal requires the sacrifice of whatever is to be served at the table. The Eucharist has always been referred to as the "sacrifice," not because Our Lord's one sacrifice is repeated but because we bring our sacrifices to be offered to the Father through his one sacrifice.

Like the wheat that has been crushed in order to become bread, we have to die to ourselves in order to be formed into Christ. Again in his Lenten Message the Pope says:

> The Son of God loved us first, while "we were yet sinners" (Rom 5:6), with an unconditional love which asks nothing in return. ... Giving not only from our abundance, but sacrificing something more in order to give to the needy, fosters that self-denial which is essential to

authentic Christian living. Strengthened by constant prayer, the baptized reveal the priority which they have given to God in their lives.[14]

At every celebration of the Eucharist we are given the opportunity to "give" of ourselves both in the way that we worship and in the way we practice stewardship.

COMMUNION IS FOSTERED AND CREATED BY OUR PARTICIPATION

The Eucharist creates communion and fosters communion. St. Paul wrote to the faithful of Corinth explaining how their divisions, reflected in their Eucharistic gatherings, contradicted what they were celebrating, the Lord's Supper. The Apostle then urged them to reflect on the true reality of the Eucharist in order to return to the spirit of fraternal communion (cf. 1 Cor 11:17–34).

—POPE JOHN PAUL II

THE BODY OF CHRIST

The Second Vatican Council captured a way of looking at our membership in the Church that is drawn from the writings of St. Paul, namely that the Church is the body of Christ. "Now you are the body of Christ and individually members of it" (1 Corinthians 12:27). The Orthodox liturgist Alexander Schmemann said:

> We need to be thoroughly aware that when we come to the temple it is not for individual prayer but to assemble together as the Church, and the visible temple itself signifies and is but an image of the temple not made by hands. Therefore, the "assembly as the Church" is in reality the first liturgical act, the foundation of the entire liturgy; and unless one understands this, one cannot understand the rest of the celebration.[15]

If we make this the backdrop to everything that we do at the Eucharist we will find that our whole view of the meaning of our acts will change. We essentially will be responding for the sustenance of our own body — which through our membership in the Church now will be Christ's body. Our voices, our movements, and our treasure will be given not to some cold institution but, as Schmemann says, to the "temple not made with hands."

FURTHER HELPS

1. Keep Your Focus on Jesus

Jesus used the image of a vine to portray the unity that exists between himself and his followers. When we are at Eucharist we become one with Christ and he promises, "If you abide in me, and my words abide in you, ask whatever you will, and it shall be done for you," (John 15:7). See the way you respond at the Eucharist as your way of abiding in Christ.

2. Learn from the Blessed Virgin Mary

Mary responded to the angel's announcement with "Let it be to me according to your word." It was beyond her understanding, but she joyously assented to God's will. All of the responses we offer at the Eucharist are to some degree beyond our comprehension. We can learn from Our Lady by putting our trust in God and responding with all of our heart to the Eucharist.

3. Foster an Attitude of Gracious Response

When Peter encountered the miracle of the Transfiguration he cried out "Lord, it is good for us to be here" (Matthew 17:4; Douay-Rheims). This is the perfect attitude for the disciple of Christ wanting to get the most out of the Eucharist. "Lord, it is good that we are here" becomes the attitude of the disciple ready to respond to whatever the Lord might ask of him or her.

4. Developing a Eucharistic Spirituality

Pope John Paul II has stated, "The Church is the Body of Christ: we walk 'with Christ' to the extent that we are in relationship 'with his body.' "[16] Examine your stance toward the body of Christ as you daily seek to follow Our Lord. Are your actions building up the body or tearing it down? Is the witness you give as part of Christ's body bringing others to Christ or turning them away?

5. A Prayer for Today

Pray the *Sucipe*, a prayer of St. Ignatius of Loyola:

> *Take, O Lord, and receive all my liberty, my memory, my understanding, and my whole will. You have given me all that I am and all that I possess: I surrender it all to You that You may dispose of it according to Your will. Give me only Your love and Your grace; with these I will be rich enough, and will have no more to desire.*

INCLINE YOUR EAR TO THE LORD

S...   *Serve*
A...   *Adore*
C...   *Confess*
R...   *Respond*
I...   Incline
F...   *Fast*
I...   *Invite*
C...   *Commune*
E...   *Evangelize*

> *Incline your ear, and hear the words of the wise, and apply your mind to my knowledge; for it will be pleasant if you keep them within you, if all of them are ready on your lips.*
>
> —PROVERBS 22:17–18

There was a commercial some years ago that featured a crowded room filled with people talking loudly suddenly becoming dead silent after someone would say in almost a whisper to another person, "My broker is E. F. Hutton, and E. F. Hutton says . . ."

The point of the advertisement was that what the broker had to say was so valuable that no other conversation mattered. Yet if we really are in tune with what is most important in life, there is nothing more important than the Word of God that we hear every time we come to the Eucharist, for what God has revealed is a path to eternal life!

It is easy to fall into the trap of thinking that when it comes to the Scriptures we've heard it all before and there is nothing new or important that is being said when we hear them proclaimed at the Eucharist. Yet if we really listen with the expectation that what we are about to hear can change our life for the better, we are in for a big surprise, one that countless people before us have experienced.

LESSONS LEARNED FROM A THREE-YEAR-OLD

Young children love to have stories read to them. They can hear the same tale repeated until they can recite it verbatim. My son has about four different storybook versions of Humpty Dumpy. He can recite the verse from memory with a few modifications of his own. He loves to sit on the edge of the sofa and fall off while being scolded that we don't want him to have to be "put back together again."

When we hear the Word of God proclaimed, we need to become like children, because no matter what our age we are always children to God. If we bring the wonderment of the child to the Eucharist we will find that no matter how often the Divine Word is heard it always has something new to say to us and has much to offer as to how we are to live.

IT'S NOT THE SAME OLD THING

St. Thomas Aquinas's notion of Scripture was that the fullness of revelation was given to the apostles. They recorded this Divine Revelation in Scripture, but when we centuries later approach the Scriptures it is accessible to us only in parts. Thus, even if we hear the same passage over and over it will always have something new to say to us because there is so much packed into the Word of God.

The truth of this is evident to anyone who opens themselves to the richness of Scripture. I have read through the entire Bible three times and have studied it for most of my adult life. I usually read the daily Mass readings in the morning and then listen to them at daily Mass. Not a day goes by that I am not struck by something in Scripture that seems so new to me that it is as though it wasn't there previously.

OUR *S*ACRIFICE

MAKE AN OFFERING OF YOUR MIND, HEART, AND EARS TO THE LORD.

We listen intently to what God has to say to us.

INCLINE YOUR EARS TO THE LORD

A question often asked of people who seek to better themselves is "Are you a listener or a 'preparing what I am going to say' type of person when it comes to conversation?" The question is a good one when it comes to the Eucharist, where God speaks to us through his Word and we can greatly benefit from what our Creator has to say to us — if we listen and let go of our thoughts about what we are going to say.

One of Jesus's best-known parables is that of the Prodigal Son. Remember that the son asked for his inheritance early (basically saying to his father, "Drop dead; I want to get on with my life") and went off and promptly squandered everything, ending up in a pigsty. Coming to his senses, the young man decided to go back to his father. As he made the journey back he rehearsed his lines: "Father I have sinned against God and you." Yet when he finally arrived home, his father welcomed him back before he could even deliver his prepared speech.

Too often we are planning our response while someone speaks, like the Prodigal who rehearsed his lines on his way home to his father. God's Word cuts through our speeches and goes right for our hearts. But we have to listen.

I remember a church that had a horrible sound system that bugged me to no end because I could barely hear what was being said. From my seat I had to bend my head toward the sanctuary and listen intently. The strange thing is that I realize that when I adopted this posture my attention was totally on what was being said and not on anything else, and thus what seemed a great difficulty at the time actually aided me in my putting my full attention on what I was hearing, albeit with difficulty.

HELP FROM THE FATHERS OF THE CHURCH

Holy Scripture is set before the eyes of the mind like a mirror, that we may see our inward person in it; for therein we learn the deformities; therein we learn the beauties that we possess; there we are made sensible of the progress that we are making; there too, we learn how far we are from proficiency.

— ST. GREGORY THE GREAT

Inclining our ears to the Lord is one way of offering the sacrifice of our thoughts in order to first listen to what God has to say. It puts us into a posture of readiness. When we hear "A reading from" we raise our level of attention because the God who created the universe is about to speak to us through his Word.

GOD'S REVELATION OF HIMSELF TO US

Now I know some reading this will find the following tidbit of anecdotal evidence a little shocking, but in the course of my experience as a teacher I have many times been asked "Where do the readings we hear at Mass come from?" Those asking the question are often shocked to hear that the readings are taken from the Bible. Not a few former Catholics have left the Catholic Church for another Church that *has* the Bible, wrongly believing that as a Catholic they had never heard the Scriptures read or proclaimed at the Eucharist.

At every celebration of the Mass we listen to readings taken from the Holy Bible. When the lector says, "A reading from St. Paul's First Letter to the Corinthians," we are listening to a selection taken from the Holy Scriptures. Just knowing this could help many Catholics to get a lot more out of the Eucharist!

The Bible contains the living word of God, which means that these readings have something to say to us right now if we are attentive. As the Catechism of the Catholic Church says, quoting the Second Vatican Council, "In the sacred books, the Father who is in heaven comes lovingly to meet his children, and talks with them" (CCC 104). In a document suggesting concrete ways that the faithful can celebrate the Year of the Eucharist (2004–2005), the Congregation of Divine Worship says that the readings we hear at the Eucharist "recall the importance of what proceeds from the mouth of God, and make us hear it not as something 'distant' from us, however inspired it may be, but as the living word by which God addresses us. We are in the context of a true 'dialogue of God and his people, a dialogue in which the marvels of salvation are proclaimed to us, and the demands of the Covenant continually re-proposed.' "[17]

HOW TO GET THE MOST OUT OF THE SCRIPTURES

If we open ourselves up to the reality that God wishes to speak to us through his Holy Word that we hear proclaimed at every Eucharistic celebration we will find that, like the disciples who had Jesus open the Scriptures to them on the road to Emmaus (see Luke 24:13–25) our "hearts will be set on fire."

What are some concrete steps we can take that will help us get the most from the Word of God? Here are a few that can easily be remembered by using the word P.R.A.Y.:

P ... Prepare
R ... Read
A ... Attend
Y ... Yield

P ... Prepare *by studying Scripture and coming to a better understanding of how Catholics approach and interpret the Word.* Pope John Paul II warned that, "If Christian individuals and families are not regularly drawing new life from the reading of the sacred text in a spirit of prayer and docility to the Church's interpretation, then it is difficult for the liturgical proclamation of the word of God alone to produce the fruit we might expect."[18] The less familiar we are with the Word that we hear proclaimed at the Eucharist, the more likely we are to be distracted by what we hear rather than fed.

R ... Read *the Mass readings beforehand.* This is something that every reader, deacon, and priest is doing in preparation for proclaiming the Word and it is something that we who listen to the proclamation could do as well, even if it is just before the start of the liturgy. If we read beforehand we can better listen when the readings are being proclaimed, and it is more likely that we will truly hear what God wishes to say to us. Consulting a good Scripture commentary is an ideal way of clearing up any confusing parts of the passages we read beforehand.

A ... Attend *to what is being read to us at the Eucharist.* Lean forward, listen intently, incline your ear toward the spoken Word. Listen to the readings in a way that acknowledges that God wishes to speak to you at this Mass. Hear God's Word addressing your concerns and your life. Pay attention when certain passages seem to jump out at you as you listen. Why do these phrases seem especially meaningful to you? Dwell on what God might be saying to you through the Mass readings. Ask yourself what God is asking you to do in response to what you have heard.

Y ... Yield *to what God is asking of you and respond with a "yes."* Every celebration of the Eucharist is a renewing of the covenant between God and us. God waits for our response. As Pope John Paul II says, "In speaking his word, God awaits our response: a response which Christ has already made for us with his 'Amen' (cf. 2 Cor 1:20–22), and which echoes in us through the Holy Spirit so that what we hear may involve us at the deepest level."[19]

HEARING THE WORD WILL CHANGE YOUR LIFE

When the people gathered in Jerusalem on the first Pentecost heard Peter proclaim the Scriptures and preach the Word (see Acts 2:14–36) it changed their lives. The Acts of the Apostles says, "Now when they heard this they were cut to the heart, and said to Peter and the rest of the apostles, 'Brethren, what shall we do?' " (Acts 2:37). Throughout the history of the Church this has happened over and over again:

- St. Antony of the Desert was converted when one day on his way to Church he was thinking of Jesus's message to the rich young man, "Go and sell all you have and give to the poor." Later when he was at the Eucharist and heard the gospel being read, it was that passage that the priest both read and preached on. St. Antony took this as a sign from God and left all his earthly possessions behind to follow Christ as a hermit in the desert.
- St. Augustine heard children playing a game where they kept repeating, "Take up and read." He picked up the Scripture and read: "Let us conduct ourselves becomingly as in the day, not in reveling and drunkenness, not in debauchery and licentiousness, not in quarreling and jealousy" (Romans 13:13). His life, too, was changed!

Chances are that you have had a similar experience in your life even if it wasn't quite so dramatic. If you haven't, chances are very good that if you incline your ear to the Lord you will. Openness to the Scriptures will change your life. You will find that you will begin to see everything that happens in your life in the new light of the gospels. There will be purpose where without God's revelation things would appear meaningless.

GREAT PREACHING!

A good friend of mine, someone who listened intently to the Word being proclaimed at Mass, once complained that at her church they weren't "being fed." I knew that she did not mean that they weren't hearing the Scriptures proclaimed or that they weren't receiving the Eucharist, because of course they were. What she was alluding to was the poor preaching that she and her fellow Catholics were being exposed to every week, while her friends at the non-Catholic church down the street were being put on the edge of their seats by their local version of a Billy Graham.

I've been to hundreds of Catholic Churches and heard as many homilies as Masses I've attended. I could count on one hand how many times I have been satiated by a great homily in my forty-six years. Yet how many times have I not been fed at Mass? Only those times when all my hopes were in the preacher and not in the Lord.

Catholics need to remember that the Lord feeds us with his Body and Blood. The bishop, priest, or deacon who preaches is not the meal, but instead is like a waiter at a restaurant, reading the menu. In this case today's special is the "same yesterday, today and tomorrow" — it is Our Lord.

A great Catholic homily should leave us famished, unsatisfied, and wanting something more. It should lead us to feel the gnawing hunger for God that only God can fill. We should see ourselves as blessed if we find the preaching of the preacher not enough, for the homilist is doing us a great service by pointing us to Christ and not at himself.

When I think about the purpose of preaching in the Catholic Church not as the end, but as a sign pointing to the end, then I can say that just about every homily I've ever heard in my life has been great!

The worst homily is the one where we feel we are ready to leave once the homilist is finished or where we feel we have been entertained — thereby becoming a spectator rather than a participant in the Eucharistic sacrifice.

FATHER, GIVE ME A WORD

In *The How-To Book of the Mass* I proposed a way to "hear" a great homily every time, namely by asking God to speak a "word" to you. In the early Church, pilgrims would make long journeys to visit holy men and women with the sole intent of asking the saint to speak a word from God to them. We can do the same, asking God to speak to us through the homilist. Really what we are doing when we approach the homily in this manner is opening ourselves up to God using his human instrument to speak to us.

I remember an incident that happened in college at Mass one day that illustrates the exact opposite of this type of openness. As we stood to sing the opening song and the student behind me noticed who was presiding at the liturgy, he bent over to whisper in my ear, "this guy has never preached a decent homily in his entire life!" I can assure you that my friend did not hear a great homily that day, even though the priest actually did preach well. It did not matter — my friend had closed himself to the experience.

As we listen to the homily, our focus should be on God and on the wonders that he can work through us weak human beings if we allow him to be God in our lives. This takes a lot of sacrificing of our ego.

KEEPING THE FOCUS ON GOD

Children often misbehave at the Eucharist because they are not the center of attention, nor should they be. Neither should any of us, yet the great mystery is that the more we focus on God in our worship the more we see the beauty of all who are created in God's image.

The greatest proclamation of the gospel that I have ever heard was from a priest who was weakened by old age and could barely be heard. Yet the humility and grace with which he read the text seemed to breathe life into the Word that he spoke and moved me greatly. God can use whatever we give him to work miracles, but we must be willing to give in order to experience them.

THE BEGINNING OF THE SPIRITUAL LIFE

Attentiveness to the word spoken is the beginning of the spiritual life. To believe Christ is to listen to his word and put it into practice. It is docility to the voice of the Holy Spirit, the interior Master who guides us to the whole truth — not only to the truth to be known, but also to the truth to be lived out.

—CONGREGATION FOR DIVINE WORSHIP AND THE DISCIPLINE OF THE SACRAMENTS

Bishop John Sheets used to describe the spiritual life as a "dialogic relationship" with God, a fancy way of saying that Christians have a spiritual life if they carry on a constant conversation with God. Any conversation demands that we both listen and respond. The Eucharist is like a nuptial ceremony where we enter into this relationship at an intense level, God speaks to us, and we respond. If we want to get the most from the Eucharist we will need to listen intently to what God has to say to us.

FURTHER HELPS

1. Keep Your Focus on Jesus

When two disciples encountered Jesus on the road to Emmaus (see Luke 24:13–27) he engaged them in conversation. He asked them what they were discussing as they journeyed. They told him and then he opened the Scriptures to them.

This is an excellent image to keep in mind when you listen to the Scriptures being proclaimed at the Eucharist. Imagine yourself in the presence of Jesus; ask him to open the Scriptures to you.

2. Learn from the Blessed Virgin Mary

When Joseph and Mary lost Jesus and found him only at the end of a three-day search, the word he spoke seemed to confuse them. Yet we are told that "His mother kept all these things in her heart." Even when the words of Jesus seemed to confuse Mary, she listened intently and "kept" his words in her heart.

We imitate the Blessed Virgin Mary by listening to the Word of God and allowing the Word to dwell in our hearts and to mold our lives. When we find it confusing or challenging we make it part of our prayer and conversation with God.

3. Fostering an Attitude of Mindfulness

When God spoke to young Samuel, he confused the voice of God with that of the prophet Eli. Finally the prophet rightly directed Samuel to say to God, "Speak, LORD, for thy servant hears" (1 Samuel 3:9). In order that we might hear what God has to say to us we must open our ears and truly listen.

4. Developing a Eucharistic Spirituality

Believe that God has something to say to you. Make an attempt to set aside times throughout the day to listen to God. Pray the Liturgy of the Hours. Read the Scriptures. Practice the art of discerning where God is in the daily events of your life. Do not be quick to judge.

5. A Prayer for Today

Practice *Lectio Divina*, sacred reading:
- *Listen intently to the proclamation of God's Word.*
- *If something strikes you during the reading, pay attention to it.*

- *What might God be telling you through this passage that strikes you?*
- *What might God be saying to you through the reading overall?*

Make the Homily part of your prayer:

- *Pray for the preacher. Ask God to bless the homilist with the Holy Spirit.*
- *Ask God to give you a "word" as you listen to the homily preached at the Eucharist.*

ℱAST IN ANTICIPATION

S...	*Serve*
A...	*Adore*
C...	*Confess*
R...	*Respond*
I...	*Incline*
ℱ...	***Fast***
I...	*Invite*
C...	*Commune*
E...	*Evangelize*

The days will come, when the bridegroom is taken away from them, and then they will fast in those days.

— LUKE 5:35

A man in the Bahamas once announced to his pastor that he was going to observe a rigorous fast during the season of Lent that year and in order to make the sacrifice even more difficult he was going to hang a smoked ham from his living room ceiling. The priest advised him against doing this, but he insisted that he wanted to make this sacrifice for the Lord.

On Good Friday the man showed up weeping quite loudly at the church doors. The priest went out to see what was causing the uproar and he met the man who had observed the severe fast. "What's wrong?" the priest asked him.

"Father, I have committed the most hideous sin," he began through the sobs. "I observed the fast throughout the season of Lent. Every day the smell of the smoked ham dangling from my ceiling grew stronger as the ocean breezes circulated in my house. Finally this morning I could stand it no longer. I grabbed a knife from the kitchen and cut the ham down and began tearing it to pieces, consuming it in a few minutes. Not only have I broken my fast but I have eaten meat on a day of abstinence."

A good friend who serves the Church in the Bahamas told me this story. Fasting is tough enough without adding to the difficulty by placing ourselves in a situation where we are surrounded by food. Perhaps this is our problem when it comes to fasting — we are always surrounded by "dangling smoked hams," things that tempt us into thinking we can be fed apart from the Eucharist.

LESSONS LEARNED FROM A THREE-YEAR-OLD

Imagine your young child feeding upon candy gathered at Halloween, from the Christmas stocking, or from the Easter basket. Are you surprised that the child has no appetite for a nourishing dinner on the days following these candy feasts?

What is the candy (the junk food) of the spiritual life? It is anything that keeps us from starving for the Bread of Life. In what do we overindulge? What good that God has given us have we turned into a "bad" because of the way we indulge in it to excess?

Every good diet program, after laying out the regiment and proposed diet, will tell the dieter to remove all forbidden foods from his or her home. Why? Because every diet guru knows that human nature is weak, and if what we need to avoid is readily within reach we are doomed to fail.

Now the purpose of fasting is spiritual. It is to cleanse us of all the false desires and appetites we have in order to enable us to focus on what is really necessary. When Jesus walked with his disciples they did not fast; there was no need to fast because they were in the presence of the Bread of Life. They found this out when they were surrounded by a crowd of thousands of people and Jesus told them to feed them (see Luke 9:10–17). They had only a few loaves of bread and some fish, and they asked him how this could possibly be enough for such a large crowd.

Jesus took what they had and blessed it, gave thanks to God for it, and told the disciples to give it to the people to eat. Everyone was satiated. Jesus said that his disciples would not fast while he was with them, but that they would fast once he had left them. Beginning in the Acts of the Apostles we see that the Christian community did fast (see Acts 13:3; 14:23).

We, too, are called to fast before receiving Our Lord in the Eucharist. Our fast prepares us for this encounter with Jesus.

OUR SACRIFICE

MAKE AN OFFERING OF ALL THAT YOU DESIRE.

We bring our hunger and thirst to the Eucharist.

HUNGRY FOR THE LORD

Older Catholics may remember a time when they would fast from midnight until they went to Mass the next morning. They would finally break their fast with a divine "breakfast," receiving Christ in the Eucharist. This practice meant that the celebration of the Eucharist was almost always held early in the morning, or if held later usually meant that almost no one received the Eucharist, since the fast would be too severe. Pope Pius XII changed this fast to three hours before Holy Communion in 1957.

In 1964 Pope Paul VI further reduced the required fast to one hour before Mass, and since then it would be fair to say that due to poor religious instruction the practice has suffered quite a bit. Recently, I attended a celebration of the Eucharist that involved a gathering of youth from Catholic schools across southern California. Moments before the Mass began, the young people seated directly in front of me were eating popcorn. Being a lifelong sinner who is quick to judge, I waited to see if the popcorn-eating youths would receive Communion. They did and I'm sure felt no compunction in doing so.

Even those who do observe the Eucharistic fast often go to great lengths to determine how to eat and drink right up to the exact moment that will be one hour before they actually receive the Eucharist. I have heard people discuss the likelihood of when Communion will be given based on the usual length of the Mass they are attending. Clearly this misses the point as much as the popcorn-munching youths or the middle-aged man judging them did.

WHAT IS THE PURPOSE OF FASTING?

Father Alexander Schmemann wrote about the fast before the Eucharist. He said that from the earliest moments of the Christian Church's history, "it had been understood as a state of *preparation* and expectation — the state of spiritual concentration on what is about to come. Physical hunger corresponds here to spiritual expectation of fulfillment, the 'opening up' of the entire human being to the approaching joy."[20]

Father Schmemann went on to say that the fast before communion is something that the individual does that joins him or her to the Church, which is always in the state of "fast," awaiting the coming of the Lord. "In the early church this total fast had a name taken from the military vocabulary; it was called *statio*, which meant a garrison in the state of alarm and mobilization. The

Church keeps 'watch' — she expects the Bridegroom and waits for Him in readiness and joy."[21]

> ## HELP FROM THE FATHERS OF THE CHURCH
> *Gluttony drove man, while reigning supreme, from paradise; abstinence recalls him from his wandering to paradise.*
>
> — ST. AMBROSE

BODY AND BLOOD FOR LIFE

We need to recapture the spiritual practice of fasting in order to be brought to our senses and recall how much we need Jesus. The type of fasting that most of us are familiar with is the type advocated by our doctor the night before we are to have our blood checked for levels of cholesterol. Our doctor is apt to warn us that we are killing ourselves with the types of food we eat. However, there is another type of fasting advocated by God and taught to us by the Church that Jesus founded that is a necessary practice in helping us to get the most from the Eucharist: "To prepare for worthy reception of this sacrament, the faithful should observe the fast required in their Church" (CCC 1387).

For Catholics of the Latin rite the fast required is spelled out in the Code of Canon Law in Canon 919. It states that a person who is to receive the Eucharist is to fast "from any food and drink" for at least one hour "before holy communion" with the exception of "water and medicine." Those who are elderly or sick and their caretakers are exempt from this law when the Eucharist is brought to them.

In the Eucharist we are fed with the Bread of Life — a food that sadly we often are not hungry enough to eat with full knowledge of the eternal benefit that is being offered to us.

I have struggled with weight as an adult, something that was absolutely not a problem when I was younger and very thin. What I have noticed about my own eating habits is that I often eat not because I am hungry but as a distraction. As I have pulled away from this habit, like a reformed alcoholic who notices how much everyone drinks, I have taken notice of how much we all tend to overeat. Archbishop Sheen once remarked that what we in the United States consider "fasting" would be "feasting" in many parts of the world!

Fasting can be the same as dieting, but the motive is not to lose bodily weight but to lose the weight of worldly concerns that weigh on us and to lighten our minds and hearts so that we can truly lift them up to the Lord. The practice of fasting and the hunger pangs that will result are apt to pull us toward the refrigerator for relief, but with focus and attention as to why we are fasting we will find that it is the resident of the tabernacle that pulls us toward him.

> *The presence of Jesus in the tabernacle must be a kind of magnetic pole attracting an ever greater number of souls enamored of him, ready to wait patiently to hear his voice and, as it were, to sense the beating of his heart. "O taste and see that the Lord is good!" (Ps 34:8).*
>
> — POPE JOHN PAUL II

When we experience hunger and sit with it we cannot help but face our needs and appetites. What is it that we think will ultimately save us? What is it that we think we cannot live without? Is it the Lord or is it someone else or some thing?

YOU DESERVE A BREAK

One of the resurrection appearances of Jesus to the apostles has Jesus grilling fish and bread on the shore of the Sea of Galilee. It is a very human image of the Son of God, one with which we can all readily identify. The apostles had been fishing all night long and had caught nothing. No doubt they were tired and they were hungry. Jesus directs them to cast their net to the "other side," where they will find some fish. They obey him and so many fish fill the net that they are unable to pull it into the boat.

Jesus then tells them, "Come and have breakfast" (John 21:12), to take a break and enjoy the meal he has prepared for them.

Our fast ends when the Lord calls us to himself. He is the Bread come down from heaven. He is the living water that will quench our thirst. He is the way, the truth, and the life!

We live in an age where we are bombarded with advertisements. They assault us at every turn on the city street, in what we hear on the airwaves, in pop-up ads on the Internet. They all promise to save us from some unsightly end, and while some can offer some relief, all of them can do so for only a time. It is the Bridegroom, Jesus, who can truly save us, and that is why fasting is so necessarily a part of the Christian life. Without it we lose sight of the fact that the real thing that we hunger and thirst for is not a thing at all, it is not some fruit hanging from a tree that is "a delight to the eyes" (Genesis 3:6), but rather the Son of God offering us salvation from the tree of the Cross.

When we bring our hunger to the Eucharist we will be fed.

FURTHER HELPS

1. Keep Your Focus on Jesus

Jesus fasted for forty days and nights before setting out on his public ministry. The gospel of Matthew says, "and afterward he was hungry" (Matthew 4:2). The devil tempted him to satisfy that hunger by turning stones into bread. Jesus rebuked Satan by quoting Scripture, "Man shall not live by bread alone, but by every word that proceeds from the mouth of God" (Matthew 4:4).

When you fast, think of Jesus fasting.

2. Learn from the Blessed Virgin Mary

Mary and Joseph made their offering in presenting Our Lord in the Temple, anticipating the Eucharist where Jesus was offered to the Father: "And when the time came for their purification according to the law of Moses, they brought him up to Jerusalem to present him to the Lord (as it is written in the law of the Lord, 'Every male that opens the womb shall be called holy to the Lord') and to offer a sacrifice according to what is said in the law of the Lord, 'a pair of turtledoves, or two young pigeons'" (Luke 2:22–24).

We imitate them in fasting, offering up our earthly hungers to the Lord to be fed by him with the Bread of Life.

3. Foster an Attitude of Fasting

Jesus instructed his disciples, "When you fast, anoint your head and wash your face, that your fasting may not be seen by men but by your Father who is in secret; and your Father who sees in secret will reward you" (Matthew 6:17–18). An attitude of fasting is motivated by a desire to come into communion with God.

4. Developing a Eucharistic Spirituality

Monitor your desires. Realize that much of what you long for cannot be gained from any material good, but God alone can satisfy. Practice mortification. Give to the poor. Help those who have emotional needs. Find penitential practices that help you to center your life on God at all times.

5. A Prayer for Today

The practice of fasting is a form of prayer.

> Fast at least one hour before you receive the Eucharist, with a special emphasis on "at least." Whenever you feel pangs of hunger, beg the Lord to feed you.

INVITE THE LORD TO COME

S...	Serve
A...	Adore
C...	Confess
R...	Respond
I...	Incline
F...	Fast
I...	**Invite**
C...	Commune
E...	Evangelize

> *Behold, I stand at the door and knock; if any one hears my voice and opens the door, I will come in to him and eat with him, and he with me.*
>
> — REVELATION 3:20

THE UNEXPECTED GUEST

In a book entitled *The God of Old*, James L. Kugel, professor of Hebrew literature at Harvard University, points out that the God of the Jewish Scriptures is a lot different than the God of popular religion. The God of "old" appeared to Abraham, Moses, and other great heroes of the Bible, and most of the time, as Professor Kugel shows, quite unexpectedly.

One of Professor Kugel's conclusions is that the world of the Scriptures is one where the material world and the spiritual world overlap. Often the meeting between God and the hero begins with the hero confusing God for another human being. Professor Kugel believes that this recognition should lead the "person of the book," that is the person who believes in the revelation given to us in the Bible, to be ever vigilant for the manifestation of God at any time and in any place.

When I read *The God of Old* I thought of the post-resurrection accounts of Jesus. Mary Magdalene encountered Jesus in the garden but didn't recognize him until he spoke her name. While fishing, Peter and John saw a stranger on the seashore cooking fish but did not recognize that it was Jesus until they had followed his fishing advice. And of course the disciples on the road to Emmaus walked seven miles with Jesus, discussing Scripture with him, and recognized that it was him only when he broke the bread.

All of this should ignite the eyes of faith with expectation. We should be ever vigilant for his coming. As Pope John Paul II says in *Ecclesia de Eucharistia*, "To contemplate Christ involves being able to recognize him wherever he manifests himself, in his many forms of presence."[22]

LESSONS LEARNED FROM A THREE-YEAR-OLD

My son Joseph loves to pick up his play phone and call his cousins Joshua and Alexandra Muse. He will engage in lively conversation with them: "Cousins, when are you going to come up and see me?" This happens so frequently that eventually I'll call my sister on a real phone, get the real cousins on the phone, and hand the phone to Joseph, who promptly gets "stage fright" and can say nothing.

I can totally relate. We spend so much time investing messianic status on people that when we actually come into their midst we are tongue-tied. I think for many, many people this is especially true when it comes to relating to God. Yet God became one of us, coming as an infant laid in a manger, a Galilean who walked the face of the earth, Jesus the Christ.

THE MESSIAH IS IN YOUR MIDST

The story is told of a monastery that had fallen on hard times.[23] The monks had grown cold in their love of God and each other.

The abbot of the monastery, worried about this sad state, decided to visit a holy hermit who lived deep in the forest and was noted for being a man of visions. The abbot presented the problems of the monastery to the holy hermit and asked for his counsel.

The hermit looked at the abbot and told him, "When you return, tell your brothers that I have seen a vision and that God has revealed to me that the Messiah is in the midst of your monastery."

The abbot went back to the monastery and relayed the message of the hermit. Suddenly life in the monastery changed. Each monk treated the others with respect and dignity, and prayers were spoken with fervor, for each monk wondered if the other might be the Messiah.

This attitude of expectation of the Lord's coming should permeate our lives as followers of Christ no matter where we are, because we know neither the day nor the hour of his coming. Yet at times it seems that we are more apt to look for signs of his absence than to listen for his knocking and entreaty to be allowed into our lives.

At the Eucharist we need to focus all of our energies on inviting the Lord to come into our lives.

OUR *Sacrifice*

MAKE AN OFFERING OF YOUR LIFE TO CHRIST.

We open ourselves up to an encounter with Jesus.

WHERE TWO OR THREE GATHER TOGETHER IN MY NAME

We may forget that the "messiah" is in our midst at every celebration of the Eucharist that we attend. Jesus promised his disciples, "Where two or three are gathered in my name, there am I in the midst of them" (Matthew 18:20). We need to be ever mindful of that.

In the Garden of Eden God searched for Adam and Eve, but in the Garden of the Empty Tomb, it was the human being, Mary Magdalene, who searched for God. We should imitate her and ever be on the lookout for Our Lord. Like the "God of Old" he will come to us, in the "least of my brethren," in the Word of God proclaimed, in the message of the homily, and in the breaking of the bread. Yet we must be vigilant and open to his coming.

One of my favorite passages in the Scriptures is in the Second Book of Kings when the King of Syria sets out to destroy Elisha the prophet. In the morning when Elisha and his servant awake they find that they are surrounded by an army of men with horses and chariots. The servant turns to Elisha and asks, "What are we going to do?" Elisha's response is:

> "Fear not, for those who are with us are more than those who are with them."
>
> Then Elisha prayed, and said, "O LORD, I pray thee, open his eyes that he may see." So the LORD opened the eyes of the young man, and he saw; and behold, the mountain was full of horses and chariots of fire round about Elisha.
>
> — 2 KINGS 6:16–17

We need to pray this prayer that the Lord might open our eyes so that we may see his presence in our midst!

EXPECTATION OF THE LORD'S COMING

The prayer of the early Church was *Maranatha* — "Come Lord Jesus." This can be our prayer as well at every moment of the day and especially when we are at the Lord's Eucharist. The words of Jesus, "If the servants knew when the Master was returning…" and "Watch, therefore, for you know not the day nor the hour," should guide our spiritual lives, because we do not know when Our Lord will come to us but we should expect that it could be at this very moment!

Fostering this expectation of the Lord's coming will enliven our faith, and we will start noticing, as Professor Kugel says, the "bigger reality" that we often are not aware is all around us.

HELP FROM THE FATHERS OF THE CHURCH

How many now say: "I wish that I could see his form, the marks of his passion, his clothes, his shoes!" But you see him, you touch him, you eat him! And you desire to see his clothes, but he gives himself to you not to see only but also touch and to eat and receive within yourself. Let no one approach it with indifference, no one fainthearted, but all burning with zeal, all fervent, all aroused.

— ST. JOHN CHRYSOSTOM

THOSE OF JESUS'S TIME

We are apt to think it would have been easier to reverence the Lord if we had lived when he walked on the face of the earth. Yet open the gospels and you will see that the people of Jesus's time had it no better than we. They found fault with his carpenter's background, with the fact that he was from Galilee, and with the fact that his Aramaic wasn't perfect.[24] Their ideas of who they thought the Messiah should be kept them from recognizing him when he was in their midst.

We risk missing Jesus time and time again if we look for the manifestation of God in all of his glory. Because God is merciful and knows we couldn't handle it, he comes to us in the imperfection of the present moment. Don't let him pass you by; invite him to come and stay with you.

FURTHER HELPS

1. Keep Your Focus on Jesus

I have an old prayer book in which there is an image of Jesus looking at the reader with the caption written under the image, "Come to me, all who labor and are heavy laden, and I will give you rest. Take my yoke upon you, and learn from me; for I am gentle and lowly in heart, and you will find rest for your souls. For my yoke is easy, and my burden is light" (Matthew 11:28–30).

Think about Jesus in this way and invite him into your life.

2. Learn from the Blessed Virgin Mary

"Blessed is she who believed that there would be a fulfillment of what was spoken to her from the Lord" (Luke 1:45). Elizabeth declared Mary to be blessed because she trusted in God's Word and opened herself to God's invitation. We imitate Mary when we too say "yes" and open ourselves up for his coming into our lives.

3. Foster an Attitude of Invitation

When Our Lord walked with two disciples on the road to Emmaus, at some point he "appeared to be going further" than they were. The more we know Jesus, the more he always seems to be going further than we are. The disciples invited him, "Stay with us" (Luke 24:29).

This is the perfect sentiment to foster in our lives, not only in the Eucharist but at all times asking the Lord to stay with us.

4. Developing a Eucharistic Spirituality

Cultivate a spirit of openness in your life to the Lord's coming under his many guises. Do not be quick to judge but do be quick to invite. Look upon every person with whom you come into contact as someone for whom Christ died and as someone who is precious in God's sight. Invite the Lord to be part of every aspect of your life.

5. A Prayer for Today

One of the earliest prayers of the Christian church was the simple prayer *Maranatha*, meaning, "Come, Lord Jesus."

> *Say "Come, Lord Jesus" frequently, inviting the Lord to come into your life.*

COMMUNE: RECEIVE THE EUCHARIST

S...	*Serve*
A...	*Adore*
C...	*Confess*
R...	*Respond*
I...	*Incline*
F...	*Fast*
I...	*Invite*
C...	**Commune**
E...	*Evangelize*

> **Abide in me, and I in you.**
>
> — JOHN 15:4

A Catholic relative asked me one day, "Why do we pray to the saints?"[25]

"Well," I answered, "we don't pray to the saints in the way that we pray to God; really what we are doing when we 'pray' to the saints is asking them to pray with and for us to God." I cited the well-known Catholic prayer the Hail Mary as an example. It includes the phrase "Holy Mary Mother of God, pray for us sinners now and at the hour of our death." "We ask Mary to 'pray for us' in this prayer," I pointed out.

Remember, Jesus said, "where two or three are gathered in my name there am I in the midst of them" (Matthew 18:20).

"Huh?" came their reply.

Why did Jesus say two or three — why not just one? It seems as though Jesus never intended for us to pray alone, and the practice of asking others to pray with us, even of invoking the followers of Christ who have fallen asleep (but are alive in Christ) to pray for us is a way for us to always pray with others even when we are physically alone.

Jesus revealed God as a communion of divine persons — the Father, the Son, and the Holy Spirit. He invited his followers to be a part of that communion. He told them, "I will not leave you desolate; I will come to you. Yet a little while, and the world will see me no more, but you will see me; because I live, you will live also. In that day you will know that I am in my Father, and you in me, and I in you" (John 14:18–20).

Entering into this communion with Jesus "where two or three are gathered in his name" is never a solitary act. It is especially difficult in a society that is as individualistic as ours is for some of us to understand this. We like to think of our faith as a private affair, something between God and the individual, but this is an illusion. To paraphrase John Donne, "No person is an island."

Before the fall there was harmony; since the fall there has been separation and division — dare we say it, individuality. Jesus has come to restore the kingdom, to bring unity. Our individuality dies in the waters of baptism. The followers of Christ make the words of St. Paul their own: "With Christ I am nailed to the cross. And

I live, now not I; but Christ lives in me" (Galatians 2:19, 20; adapted from Douay-Rheims).

> ### HELP FROM THE FATHERS OF THE CHURCH
> *Just as when one mixes melted wax with other melted wax, a united whole results, so by the communion of the body and blood of Christ, he is in us, and we are in him.*
>
> — ST. CYRIL OF ALEXANDRIA

If you walk into an empty Catholic church building you will usually have an experience of not being alone. First the glimmering sanctuary lamp signals that Christ is present in the Blessed Sacrament that resides in the tabernacle. Second, the images of saints call to mind those who have passed from this earthly life and live with Christ in heaven but who are still very concerned about what is going on here (see Revelation 6:9–11). Then there are the images of angels that call to mind the ministering force of unseen spirits that constantly surround us (see 2 Kings 6:15–17). Finally there are those who have died and are still in a state of purgation asking for our prayers.

Every time we gather for the Eucharist we enter into a communion with the whole church: those present with us, those who are far off, and those who have gone before us in Christ, both those in purgatory and those in heaven. Traditionally these three groups were called the Church militant (those of us still on earth), the Church suffering (those in purgatory), and the Church victorious (those in Heaven). The Church is a communion with Christ, and every celebration of the Eucharist brings about this communion and maintains it.

If you want to get the most out of the Eucharist you will need to offer yourself, "die to yourself," and enter into communion with Christ and his body.

OUR *Sacrifice*

MAKE AN OFFERING OF YOURSELF TO THE BODY OF CHRIST.

We die to ourselves so that Christ might live within us.

HOW DO YOU RECEIVE THE EUCHARIST?

At the opening of the Eucharistic Congress that initiated the Year of the Eucharist in 2004, Cardinal Jozef Tomko, in his homily, said, "Ask who the Eucharist is, not what the Eucharist is." The Eucharist is above all an encounter with Jesus Christ. Do we receive the Eucharist as a precious gift of communion with our Divine Savior or do we take it without reflecting on whom it is that we are touching?

There was a woman who had a serious health problem (see Luke 8:42–48). She had been to any number of doctors, none of whom had been able to help her. She had heard about someone named Jesus of Nazareth who was working great miracles, and seeing a crowd gathering around the wonder worker, she made her way toward him. Something within her made her believe that if she could just touch the hem of his garment she would be healed of her illness. Working her way through the crowd, she nudged her way to Jesus. People were pressing in on him from every side, but reaching out she finally managed to touch him, just barely.

Jesus stopped and looked around, asking, "Who touched me?" His disciples pointed out to him that everyone was touching him. Yet although there were many around him, pressing in on him and touching him, no one but the woman who had reached out in faith had truly touched him.

When we acknowledge our weakness and reach out to receive the Lord we will experience the Lord Jesus in the way that the woman who touched him in the crowd did. Have you lost sight of "who" the Eucharist is? Are you reaching out in faith to touch Jesus when you receive him?

LESSONS LEARNED FROM A THREE-YEAR-OLD

My son dutifully follows behind me every Sunday as our family processes toward the altar to receive the Eucharist. He folds his hands, and usually bumps into me every time the line stops. He watches me bow and receive the Eucharist, then when it is his turn sometimes he receives a blessing — sometimes nothing. Many times he reaches out and attempts to take the Eucharist from the priest.

It is touching to watch this, and always causes me to reflect on how mindful I am of what I'm being allowed to receive.

A lot of churches have a sign that hangs on the wall where the priest vests for Mass that reads, "Celebrate this Mass as though it were your first" — it is an admonition for the priest to preside with the zeal and devotion that he had when he was first ordained. I remember a priest saying in a homily once that he hated those signs because he would never want to celebrate the Eucharist the way he had the first time because he was so nervous that he doubted he had done it validly! Still, the wisdom behind the admonition is clear: Bring your faith in Jesus to this Mass you celebrate.

I think there should be a similar sign at the entrance of every church for the rest of us to encounter every time we approach the altar to receive the Eucharist:

Receive Our Lord Jesus Christ like this is your first Holy Communion.

This would mean approaching the altar with the mind of a seven-year-old child again (for those of us who are cradle Catholics) — not necessarily a bad thing when we consider that Jesus said, "Unless you turn and become like children, you will never enter the kingdom of heaven" (Matthew 18:3).

JESUS RECEIVES US AT COMMUNION

The woman who reached out to touch Jesus wanted to do it with some degree of anonymity — not unlike the way most of us are at Mass. Yet Jesus wouldn't let her get away that easily; he summoned her from the crowd, and then, receiving her, sent her in peace (see Luke 8:48). Pope John Paul II has pointed out that not only do we receive Christ at the Eucharist but that Jesus also "receives us":

> Incorporation into Christ, which is brought about by Baptism, is constantly renewed and consolidated by sharing in the Eucharistic Sacrifice, especially by that full sharing which takes place in sacramental communion. We can say not only that *each of us receives Christ*, but also that *Christ receives each of us*. He enters into friendship with us: "You are my friends" (Jn 15:14). Indeed, it is because of him that we have life: "He who eats me will live because of me" (Jn 6:57). Eucharistic communion brings about in a sublime way the mutual "abiding" of Christ and each of his followers: "Abide in me, and I in you" (Jn 15:4).[26]

Both receiving Christ and being received by Jesus should change us. This exchange "enables us to have a certain foretaste of heaven on earth."[27]

THE IDEAL OF COMMUNION

The model for the communion that we seek in the Eucharist is exhibited in the second chapter of the Acts of the Apostles. The early believers who had been baptized, we are told, "devoted themselves to the apostles' teaching and fellowship, to the breaking of bread and the prayers" (Acts 2:42). This is a description of the celebration of the Eucharist, where we gather to hear the gospel that has been handed down to us by the apostles and to hear the preaching of those who trace their priesthood back to the apostles. We share in the prayers and the breaking of the Eucharistic bread. Yet there is a further aspect of this communion: "all who believed were together and had all things in common; and they sold their possessions and goods and distributed them to all, as any had need"(Acts 2:44–45).

Pope John Paul says, "At each Holy Mass we are called to measure ourselves against the ideal of communion which the Acts of the Apostles paints as a model for the Church in every age."[28] This examination of our level of communion consists of four elements. We must be:

1. Gathered around the Apostles

Jesus chose twelve disciples that he called apostles. He set them over his Church. The apostles, in turn, appointed successors to pass on what the Lord had taught them to future believers. The pope and the bishops are the apostles that we gather around today. They teach the truth that has been handed down to them by Christ. Being "in communion" with Our Lord means that we accept what the Church teaches through the apostles as true. Dying to oneself and accepting this truth is a necessary condition for truly accepting Christ.

2. Called by the Word of God

Each of us is called into this communion by God's Word that summons all to "come to him." Accepting this call means turning away from the fallen world and toward Christ's view of the world; it means that we must, as St. Paul said to the Philippians, "Do nothing from selfishness or conceit, but in humility count others better than yourselves. Let each of you look not only to his own interests but also to the interests of others. Have this mind among yourselves, which is yours in Christ Jesus" (Philippians 2:3–5). God's Word forms the mind of Christ within each of us.

3. Capable of Sharing Spiritual Goods

We are called to share the spiritual riches that we are freely given by Christ. We do this by praying for those who are in need of conversion, who have fallen away, and who are ignorant of the truth. Rather than judging we must turn to Christ and believe in his power to change the hardest heart of stone into a heart of flesh. We must pray for the dead, having Masses offered for their sake and "offering up" our own sufferings on their behalf — we cannot forget the intimate communion that we share with the deceased members of the body of Christ.

4. Sharing in Material Goods

Like the first followers of Christ who shared with all who were in need, we are called to share our material wealth with those who are without. We cannot ignore the Lazarus's at our gate while we feast splendidly at the Lord's table (see Luke 16:9–31). The truth-fulness of what we do when we come to the Eucharist is exhibited by how we are transformed. The Pope states: "We cannot delude ourselves: by our mutual love and, in particular, by our concern for those in need we will be recognized as true followers of Christ (cf. Jn 13:35; Mt. 25:31-46). This will be the criterion by which the authenticity of our Eucharistic celebrations is judged."[29]

MEDICINE OF IMMORTALITY

St. Ignatius of Antioch was a bishop who was arrested and then taken from Syria to Rome, where he was put to death for his faith. Along his journey to Rome, he wrote letters to the local churches. In his letter to the Ephesians he has a unique way of describing the Eucharist. He calls the Eucharist the "medicine of immortality," saying that it is the "antidote which wards off death but yields continuous life in union with Jesus Christ."[30]

Without Jesus Christ we are all terminally ill; how much time we have left may differ, but without him the end is certain. Yet Our Lord does not desire our destruction and offers us eternal life. When we come to receive the Eucharist and believe in the power of the Lord to ward off all of our death-induced behaviors and to help us to live as members of the kingdom of heaven, we truly will get the most out of the Eucharist. He will live in us and we in communion with him.

FURTHER HELPS

1. Keep Your Focus on Jesus

The image of Jesus on the cross, giving his life for our sins and the image of Jesus at table with his disciples are two parallel thoughts that can help us focus on the communion that we seek with the Lord. We have to die to ourselves, to have the mind of Christ, and to live for God and one another. Just as Jesus gave his life on the cross and shared that life in the bread and wine he offered at the Last Supper, so will he continue to give through us when we truly enter into communion with him.

2. Learn from the Blessed Virgin Mary

"When Jesus saw his mother, and the disciple whom he loved standing near, he said to his mother, 'Woman, behold, your son!' Then he said to the disciple, 'Behold, your mother!' And from that hour the disciple took her to his own home" (John 19:26–27). At the foot of the cross Mary and the beloved disciple formed the first Christian community.

When we receive Christ we become one with our brothers and sisters. Jesus entrusts them to us. We should ask our Mother Mary to help us love our brothers and sisters in the way that Jesus asks us to.

3. Foster an Attitude of Communion

When Jesus announced himself as the Bread of Life, the people said, "Lord, give us this bread always" (John 6:34). Desiring the Bread of Life above all is a sure way for us to respond to Our Lord's call to "abide in him." We need to realize that our very life depends entirely upon communion with him.

4. Developing a Eucharistic Spirituality

Let your "Amen" to the "Body of Christ" foster a perpetual "Amen" to every moment of life that God gives you. Bear witness to the reality that every moment of your life depends upon God's gift of life. Never forget God's place in your home, work, or recreation.

Let your communion with God in the Eucharist extend to every area of your life.

5. A Prayer for Today

This prayer, "The Breastplate of St. Patrick," was written by St. Patrick:

> *Christ ever with me, Christ before me, Christ behind me*
> *Christ within me, Christ beneath me, Christ above me*
> *Christ to my right side, Christ to my left side*
> *Christ in his breadth, Christ in his length, Christ in depth*
> *Christ in the heart of every man who thinks of me*
> *Christ in the mouth of every man who speaks to me*
> *Christ in every eye that sees me*
> *Christ in every ear that hears me.*

ℰVANGELIZE: SHARE THE GOOD NEWS!

S...	*Serve*
A...	*Adore*
C...	*Confess*
R...	*Respond*
I...	*Incline*
F...	*Fast*
I...	*Invite*
C...	*Commune*
ℰ...	**Evangelize**

And preach as you go, saying, "The kingdom of heaven is at hand."

— MATTHEW 10:7

AN URGENT SUMMONS

One day after I had finished a talk on the Emmaus story, using it as a model for every celebration of the Eucharist (see *The How-To Book of the Mass*), a young priest came up to me. He said, "It sounds like I shouldn't be standing at the back of the church greeting people as they leave but instead should be out in the road, directing traffic to help everyone get out of the parking lot as soon as possible."

I smiled at his keen observation.

At every Eucharist we have experienced something that needs to be shared with the world. Pope John Paul II has recently emphasized this, saying: "The two disciples of Emmaus, upon recognizing the Lord, 'set out immediately' (cf. Luke 24:33), in order to report what they had seen and heard. Once we have truly met the Risen One by partaking of his body and blood, we cannot keep to ourselves the joy we have experienced. The encounter with Christ, constantly intensified and deepened in the Eucharist, issues in the Church and in every Christian *an urgent summons to testimony and evangelization.*"[31]

One of the greatest threats to getting the most out of the Eucharist is to think what we get in hearing the Word proclaimed and in receiving the Lord in the breaking of the bread is meant only for us and not to be shared.

Do you remember Jesus's Parable of the Talents (see Matthew 25:14–30)? Jesus tells of a man who is going on a journey and entrusts his wealth to three servants. Two take what they have been given and double the value. One buries what he has been given. If you are like me, you tend to focus on this poor chap who is soundly condemned at the end of the story and has what was entrusted to him taken from him and given to someone else. Yet look at the other two; both are praised for using what they had been given and told to "enter into the joy" of their master, God.

When we approach the Eucharist with the attitude of a servant being entrusted with a gift, we cannot help but reflect on this parable and ask ourselves what our attitude is toward the gift entrusted to us in the Eucharist. Are we fearful or filled with trust? Do we bury the gift or share Our Lord with others?

LESSONS LEARNED FROM A THREE-YEAR-OLD

We have this little ritual that we go through every Sunday in our home. My son will ask, "What day is it?"

I tell him, "It's Sunday."

"What means Sunday?" he replies.

"Church day," I tell him.

"I don't want to go to Church," he whines (this is why even from birth it requires a sacrifice to get the most from the Eucharist).

Now the easiest thing for me to do would be to say, "Okay, you don't have to go." I've even seen this advocated by some who find children a "distraction" at Mass. Yet when I look at my three-year-old I think of a foundation that is being laid in his life. I think of the gift of faith that my parents gave me that has prepared me for everything life has dealt me. I want my child's life to be built upon rock so that whatever storms he may face will not destroy him later in life.

What my three-year-old teaches me is that the people I really love and care about are those I want to experience the saving power of the Eucharist. That's why he goes to Mass whether he wants to or not — and that's why I go whether I want to or not. When his mother Amy and I presented him for baptism we promised we would bring him up in the faith. We take that charge seriously.

"Can we go to the doughnut church?" he asks, referring to a church that sporadically offers coffee, juice, and doughnuts after Mass (and once a year even offers imported German beer and bratwurst).

My son doesn't have much choice in the matter right now, but how he acts when we arrive at the church is another issue.

If we go to this church and he spots the aforementioned doughnut boxes on a table in the nave of the church, we have a bargaining chip: "You get one only if you are good!"

Now he will sacrifice throughout the celebration of the Eucharist for that promised doughnut. I think watching this is the genesis of this entire book. For a young person it might be a doughnut that merits sacrifice, but hopefully as adults we have graduated beyond wanting to go to the "doughnut" church to wanting to attend the church that offers the Bread of Life.

Jesus said, "I am the bread of life; he who comes to me shall not hunger, and he who believes in me shall never thirst" (John 6:35). Everything else that we hunger for and desire in the end leaves us hungering and desiring for more — but Jesus offers us and everyone on the face of the earth an end to our hunger and thirst.

OUR *Sacrifice*

MAKE AN OFFERING OF WHAT YOU RECEIVE IN THE EUCHARIST.

We take the gift of Jesus and share it with others.

A MATTER OF LIFE AND DEATH

Think of how many people you have known personally who have lived horrible lives because they aimlessly followed one false god after another. How many lives have been destroyed by addictions because there was never anyone to intervene and point them toward a higher power who could rescue them? How many young people are plunging themselves into the false gospel of the world with all of its pomp and empty promises, setting themselves up for a meaningless existence? Do you and I have anything to offer these people? Do we love them like we love our own children?

Back in the 1950s an incident happened in the divided city of Berlin. A group from East Berlin drove a garbage truck into West Berlin and dumped it in the streets, leaving a sign: "A gift from East Berlin." A group of outraged citizens from West Berlin decided to answer this insult in a unique way. They loaded up a truck with food and gifts for children and under cover of darkness unloaded the goods in a street in East Berlin, leaving a sign: "A Gift from West Berlin: One gives what one *has* to give."

What are we giving to our family, friends, and co-workers? Do we realize the treasure that we have been given begs to be shared with others?

I suspect what keeps many of us from sharing our faith with others is a fear that we might appear to be imposing our beliefs on them. Yet do we feel that way when it comes to sharing our pleasure with a type of food, a favorite television show or movie, or a particular product that we find helpful?

Pope John Paul II has said, "We should not be afraid to speak about God and to bear proud witness to our faith."[32] Jesus told his disciples, "Do not be anxious how or what you are to answer or what you are to say; for the Holy Spirit will teach you in that very hour what you ought to say" (Luke 12:11–12), when called to testify to their faith.

How we witness the faith should always follow the example of Jesus. Sadly, some of the worst examples of well-meaning people following the wrong path have been the attempts to force people to convert. Pope John Paul II remarks, "One who learns to say 'thank you' in the manner of the crucified Christ might end up as a martyr, but never as a persecutor."[33]

Go . . .

Pope John Paul II notes, "The dismissal at the end of each Mass is *a charge* given to Christians, inviting them to work for the spread of the gospel and the imbuing of society with Christian values."[34] The word *Mass* is derived from the Latin dismissal *ite missa est* that literally means, "Go, you are sent." The communion that we experience with God at the Eucharist sustains and prepares us for a mission — to bring Christ to the world!

The final words of Jesus in three of the four gospels contain the word "Go." Only Luke's gospel is missing this admonition from Jesus but it contains a counsel to prepare the followers of

Christ before they "go." A look at the final mission that is given to the disciples might help us discern where we might be called to go and share what we have been given.

Luke's "Stay"

> Thus it is written, that the Christ should suffer and on the third day rise from the dead, and that repentance and forgiveness of sins should be preached in his name to all nations, beginning from Jerusalem. You are witnesses of these things. And behold, I send the promise of my Father upon you; but *stay* in the city, *until you are clothed with power from on high.*
>
> — LUKE 24:46–49 (EMPHASIS ADDED)

The mission we have in Christ begins with our communion with him brought about by the work of the Holy Spirit. "Stay … until you have been clothed with power from on high," is the prerequisite to our going forth. We can't share what we don't have. We should call upon the grace of our baptism and confirmation that the Spirit might empower us to "go" forth and share Christ with others.

Matthew's "Go"

> And Jesus came and said to them, "All authority in heaven and on earth has been given to me. *Go therefore and make disciples of all nations*, baptizing them in the name of the Father and of the Son and of the Holy Spirit, teaching them to observe all that I have commanded you; and lo, I am with you always, to the close of the age."
>
> — MATTHEW 28:18–20 (EMPHASIS ADDED)

Now you might be tempted to think that this "go" is just for the clergy; after all, it requires teaching and baptizing. Yet if you are up on your basic Catholic beliefs you will recall that:

- "In case of necessity, any person can baptize provided that he have the intention of doing that which the Church does and provided that he pours water on the candidate's head while saying: 'I baptize you in the name of the Father, and of the Son, and of the Holy Spirit'" (CCC 1284).
- "Since, like all the faithful, lay Christians are entrusted by God with the apostolate by virtue of their Baptism and Confirmation, they have the right and duty, individually or grouped in associations, to work so that the divine message of salvation may be known and accepted by all men throughout the earth. This duty is the more pressing when it is only through them that men can hear the Gospel and know Christ. Their activity in ecclesial communities is so necessary that, for the most part, the apostolate of the pastors cannot be fully effective without it" (CCC 900).

Clearly this shows that everyone is called to evangelize the world. We all touch different people, and our Lord commands us to spread the Good News to those whom God places in our path.

Mark's "Go"

And entering the tomb, they saw a young man sitting on the right side, dressed in a white robe; and they were amazed. And he said to them, "Do not be amazed; you seek Jesus of Nazareth, who was crucified. He has risen, he is not here; see the place where they laid him. *But go, tell his disciples and Peter that he is going before you to Galilee*; there you will see him, as he told you."

— MARK 16:5–7 (EMPHASIS ADDED)

Here the women who come to the tomb are commissioned to tell the apostles that Jesus is going ahead of them to Galilee. Galilee was their home.

We are all called to enthrone Christ in our homes — our Galilee. We cannot live our faith like it is something that we use only when we are in church. The Lord we receive in the Eucharist comes home with us. If we live our lives at home with this belief, "there we will see him." We will see him in our spouse. We will see him in our children. We will see him in our parents and in-laws. When we seek him out in our family members, they will see him in our actions.

John's "Go"

> [Jesus] said to him the third time, "Simon, son of John, do you love me?" Peter was grieved because he said to him the third time, "Do you love me?" And he said to him, "Lord, you know everything; you know that I love you." Jesus said to him, "Feed my sheep. Truly, truly, I say to you, *when you were young, you girded yourself and walked where you would; but when you are old, you will stretch out your hands, and another will gird you and carry you where you do not wish to go.*" (This he said to show by what death he was to glorify God.) And after this he said to him, "Follow me."
>
> —JOHN 21:17–19 (EMPHASIS ADDED)

Perhaps of all the "go's" at the end of Jesus's earthly ministry, this one is the one we least want to hear. We do not like to hear that Our Lord is sending us where we "do not wish to go." Yet, if we love him, we will follow him, no matter where that takes us. Following Christ means doing what Christ wants us to do. We must ask him to show us his will, fearless of what we might hear.

Life seldom goes according to our plans. A terrible accident nearly took Father Benedict Groeschel's life in 2004. At the beginning of *There Are No Accidents*, a book in which Father Groeschel discerns what God's will was in this unfortunate event, one will find the verses from John's gospel quoted here. The witness of our faith speaks loudly and often without words when the storm comes and beats against the rock of the foundation upon which our lives of faith are built.

BEING CHRIST TO ONE ANOTHER

The Mass should transform us into Christ. People should want to follow him because of what they encounter when they are with us.

There was once a missionary who was lost at sea who by chance washed up on the shore where there was a remote native village. Half-dead from starvation, exposure, and seawater, he was found by the people of the village and was nursed back to full health. Subsequently, he lived among these people for twenty years. During that whole time he confessed no faith to them, he preached no sermons, he read them no Scripture. Yet when they were sick, he attended to them, sitting long into the night. When people were hungry, he gave them food. When people were lonely, he was a source of company. He taught the ignorant. He was a source of enlightenment to those who were more knowledgeable. He always took the side of those who had been wronged. There was not a single human condition with which he did not identify.

After twenty years had passed, missionaries came from the sea to the village and began talking to the people about a man called Jesus, and after hearing of Jesus, the natives insisted that he had lived among them for the past twenty years. "Come, we will introduce you to the man about whom you have been speaking." The missionaries were led to a hut, and there they found their long-lost fellow missionary who they had thought dead.[35]

As St. Francis said, "Preach the Gospel, if necessary use words."

A FORETASTE OF HEAVEN

What Our Lord offers us surpasses our wildest dreams. St. Paul tells us that "Eye has not seen nor ear heard, nor has it entered into the heart of man, what things God has prepared for those who love him" (1 Corinthians 2:9, Challoner-Rheims).

This is our final end, and every Eucharist gives us a foretaste of heaven. Pope John Paul II has said that this aspect of what we celebrate in the Eucharist, although focused on the future, "commits us to our mission here":

> The Eucharist is truly a glimpse of heaven appearing on earth. It is a glorious ray of the heavenly Jerusalem which pierces the clouds of our history and lights up our journey. A significant consequence of the eschatological tension inherent in the Eucharist is also the fact that it spurs us on our journey through history and plants a seed of living hope in our daily commitment to the work before us. Certainly the Christian vision leads to the expectation of "new heavens" and "a new earth" (Rev 21:1), but this increases, rather than lessens, our sense of responsibility for the world today. I wish to reaffirm this forcefully at the beginning of the new millennium, so that Christians will feel more obliged than ever not to neglect their duties as citizens in this world. Theirs is the task of contributing with the light of the Gospel to the building of a more human world, a world fully in harmony with God's plan.[36]

The heaven that we experience when God is our priority is something to share. Call to mind the great saints to see how much can be accomplished by one person clothed in the power of God!

We are all called to be saints, but our sainthood extends only so far as we trust in Christ.

FURTHER HELPS

1. Keep Your Focus on Jesus

Open the gospels and witness how Jesus brought the "Good News" to the people. Observe and imitate Jesus's way of evangelizing others. Ask the Holy Spirit for the words to speak to all whom God places in your life.

2. Learn from the Blessed Virgin Mary

"His mother said to the servants, 'Do whatever he tells you' " (John 2:5). We begin as servants and we go forth as servants, doing what the Blessed Virgin Mary asks of us: "Do whatever Jesus tells you." We must take his message out into our homes and workplaces, proclaiming the one who can change the water of humanity into the wine of divinity.

3. Foster an Attitude of Evangelization

Jesus said, "Do not be anxious how you are to speak or what you are to say; for what you are to say will be given to you in that hour; for it is not you who speak, but the Spirit of your Father speaking through you" (Matthew 10:19–20). We should trust that the Spirit will give us the words we are to speak when witnessing to the power of Christ in our lives to others.

4. Developing a Eucharistic Spirituality

Pope John Paul II has said, "We should not be afraid to speak about God and to bear proud witness to our faith."[37] Share your faith with those whom God places in your life. See life not as a series of accidents but as a series of meaningful events and opportunities given to you by God.

5. A Prayer for Today

The following is a prayer that was prayed every day by Cardinal Mercier. He called it "A Secret of Sanctity" and promised that anyone who prayed it every day would find his or her life changed.

> *O Holy Spirit, Soul of my soul, I adore You. Enlighten, guide, strengthen and console me. Tell me what I ought to do and command me to do it. I promise to be submissive in everything that You permit to happen to me, only show me what is Your will.*

APPENDIX

How to Get the Most Out of the Eucharist
When You Cannot Receive Holy Communion

At the beginning of this book I mentioned a man who attended the Eucharist for many years with his Catholic wife. He never received the Eucharist in all of those years. He had been raised a Presbyterian and did not wish to convert until he was in the last months of his life. It is my belief that in all of those years that he attended the Eucharist, although not receiving Communion, he was nonetheless receiving great graces from God that prepared him for his personal time of crisis.

There are many who attend the Eucharist who are not able to receive Holy Communion. They include:

- Children who have not reached the age of reason
- Catholics in need of the Sacrament of Reconciliation
- Catholics who are in an irregular marriage
- Baptized Christians who are not Catholic but attend:
    - To support their spouse and family
    - To attend a funeral, wedding, or some other celebration
    - To learn more about the Catholic Church
- Non-Christians who may attend for any of the same reasons as stated for baptized Christians

If you are in any one of these groups (excluding children) I would encourage you strongly to make an appointment with your parish priest to discern whether there is any way for you to be reconciled. Many people find, no matter what their situation, that exclusion from the Eucharist can be remedied (no matter what your Catholic relatives or friends might tell you), and in some cases people find that they could have been receiving the Eucharist all along.

If after meeting with a priest you find that there is still something blocking you from receiving the Eucharist or that it will take some time to remedy, please do not feel that there is no reason for you to attend the Eucharist. As with the man who attended Mass for years before ever receiving Holy Communion, an encounter with Jesus is not only a possibility but a certainty, guaranteed just by your presence where "two or more are gathered" in his name.

LESSONS LEARNED FROM A THREE-YEAR-OLD

Every Catholic has spent part of his or her life as a Catholic attending the Eucharist without receiving Holy Communion. I am reminded of that every time I have my three-year-old son with me at Mass. He dutifully follows me up to receive, walking, with his hands folded, between his mother and me. Sometimes he'll receive a blessing (there are some Catholic Churches that offer this to people of all ages who cannot receive the Eucharist, but this is the personal initiative of the priest), while at other times he gets nothing other than a practice run for the day when he will be able to receive the Eucharist himself.

Yet he still goes, and the reason that we have brought him to Mass from the time he was an infant is that we believe in the transforming power of the Eucharist. Just being in the presence of Christ in the person of the priest, the gathered body of Christ, the Word of God proclaimed, and his Real Presence in the Eucharist offers him many ways to come to know Jesus and to both receive him and be received by him. Simply think of Our Lord beckoning the children to come to him and blessing them.

This blessing of Christ is given to everyone who is present at the Eucharist. No one is excluded from this blessing, and we shouldn't downplay its effect in our lives.

OUR *S*ACRIFICE

MAKE AN OFFERING OF YOUR
S.A.C.R.I.F.I.C.E.

We take the blessing of Christ and strive to follow him more closely.

The key to getting the most out of the Eucharist if you can't receive Holy Communion is a slight variation of the same principles that I've attached to the word *sacrifice*; namely, to Serve, Adore, Confess, Respond, Incline, Fast, Invite, Commune, and Evangelize.

SERVE

My friend who accompanied his wife for over thirty years to the Eucharist brought an attitude of service to the Eucharist. He volunteered to be an usher. It gave him a way to actively participate. Now, depending upon your situation, getting involved by being an usher, a cantor, a member of the choir, or participating in the Rites for full communion or Christian Initiation are all ways to take a more active role in the Eucharist, especially when you are unable to receive the Eucharist.

You will come to the Eucharist with a sense of purpose and an attitude of service to God that will greatly enhance your experience.

ADORE

Focusing on God is paramount to our experience of the Eucharist. We are there because we believe that God has given us everything we possess. We owe God our worship. We keep the focus on Jesus's revelation that what we do in the Eucharist was entrusted by Jesus as the way that God wishes for us to offer him worship.

Too often those who are excluded from receiving the Eucharist tend over time to separate Jesus from the Church. We need to keep in mind that although the Church is made up of us sinners, it transcends any one of us and is the way that God has chosen for us to commune with him. Offering God adoration is an excellent way to keep the fire of God's love burning in our hearts.

CONFESS

Confessing that all our trust is in God enlightens us as to how we have failed to truly trust in his love in our lives. There are some who could once again present themselves to the Eucharist if they would only present themselves to a priest in the Sacrament of Penance and Reconciliation. If this is your situation, by all means reconcile yourself. There is nothing that you have done that God cannot forgive.

What blocks many of us is our pride. We do not like to admit our weakness. Like the Prodigal Son, we may have sold our inheritance for something that can never bring us lasting love and peace. May God give us the wisdom to rise and turn back to the Father who waits for our return.

No matter what our situation, coming to the Eucharist with an attitude of humility along with a trust that God can save us will guarantee that we will be fed even if we physically cannot receive his Body and Blood.

RESPOND

Participating in the Eucharist by responding by word and gesture calls to mind that we are part of the body of Christ. In doing this we partake in a communion that we may experience only in retrospect. I remember a middle-aged woman telling me that she had been attending a Catholic Church for years before she even thought of becoming a Catholic, and that on the day of her reception into the Church she realized that it was the culmination of a communion that had been building over the many years she had responded with the rest of the body of Christ at the Eucharist.

INCLINE

The Word of God is one way that we all can experience a communion with Christ. Knowing that we are hearing the Word of

God at the Eucharist, believing in the power of God to speak from the proclaimed Word, is a way to enjoy the presence of Christ. In fact, as with someone deprived of one of their faculties it seems that focusing on the Word takes on a special urgency when we cannot receive him in Holy Communion. In the fuller sense of the word *Eucharist* — meaning the entire celebration of Mass — God's Word is one way that we can always receive Christ.

It is the first step to understanding our situation in the light of Christ. Ask yourself, "What action does hearing the Word of God inspire within me?"

FAST

Although the Church does not require a fast for those who are not receiving the Eucharist, if we who are in a situation such that we cannot receive Communion want to get the most from the Eucharist, we will still observe the fast. In doing so we will prepare our hearts, begging the Lord to satisfy our hunger, which will be made more apparent by our participation in the Eucharistic fast.

INVITE

We need the Lord! Inviting him into our hearts is something that we need to do at all times. Like Zachaeus, we long to hear the Lord say, "Come down from that tree, for I will dine with you today" (see Luke 19:5). We repeat with the disciples on the road to Emmaus, "Stay with us, Lord" (see Luke 24:29). Beg the Lord to come to you, and believe that he desires to be in communion with you.

COMMUNE

When others go forward to receive Communion, do not neglect to make a spiritual communion. You can memorize a traditional form such as that included here, or speak a prayer of your own creation telling the Lord how much you desire to be in union with him and his Church.

My Jesus, I believe that you are present in the Most Holy Sacrament. I love you above all things, and I desire to receive you into my soul. Since I cannot at this moment receive you sacramentally, come at least spiritually into my heart. I embrace you as if you were already there and unite myself wholly to you. Never permit me to be separated from you. Amen.

EVANGELIZE

You need to share the Good News of Jesus Christ just like everyone else. Make it a priority; perhaps God has allowed your current situation so that you may help others like yourself in need of his love. Often by ministering to others we come to a better understanding of who God is and the power of his love to overcome any obstacle that we might be placing in the way of experiencing his love to the fullest in our lives.

KEEP THE FAITH

I know good and holy people who have attended the Eucharist for years without the benefit of receiving the Eucharist. Their faith has inspired many. Their witness has caused many a flippant Catholic to examine his or her own commitment to the Faith. It is all about God; remember that and you will get more and more from the Eucharist as time passes.

NOTES

1. Pope John Paul II, *Ecclesia de Eucharistia*, 10.
2. Ibid., 13.
3. Alexander Schmemann, *The Eucharist*, 23.
4. Pope John Paul II, *Ecclesia de Eucharistia*, 53.
5. From the Rite of Ordination of a Priest (emphasis added).
6. Pope John Paul II, *Mane Nobiscum Domine*, 28.
7. Benedict of Nursia, *Rule of St. Benedict*, XX.
8. St. Augustine, *Soliloquies*, Book 1:5.
9. Benedict of Nursia, *Rule of St. Benedict*, IV, 21.
10. Alexander Schmemann, *Journals of Father Alexander Schmemann, 1973–1983* (translated by Julianna Schmemann), St. Vladimir's Seminary Press, Crestwood, N.Y., 2002, 133.
11. Congregation for Divine Worship and the Discipline of the Sacraments, *The Year of the Eucharist: Suggestions and Proposals*, 22.
12. Illustrations Unlimited (James S. Hewett, editor), Tyndale House Publishers, Inc. Wheaton, Ill., 1998 (attributed to Mark Link, S.J.), 422.
13. Pope John Paul II, *Message of His Holiness for Lent 2003*, 3.
14. Ibid., 4.
15. Alexander Schememann, *The Eucharist*, 23.
16. Pope John Paul II, *Mane Nobiscum Domine*, 20.
17. Congregation for Divine Worship and the Discipline of the Sacraments, *The Year of the Eucharist: Suggestions and Proposals*, 21.
18. Pope John Paul II, *Dies Domini*, 40.

19. Ibid., 41.
20. Alexander Schmemann, *Great Lent: Journey to the Pascha*, St. Vladimir's Seminary Press, Crestwood, N.Y., 1969, 49.
21. Ibid., 50.
22. Pope John Paul II, *Ecclesia de Eucharistia*, 6.
23. The Reverend Kevin McGee used the story in a sermon some years ago and I have never forgotten it — a testament to the quality of his preaching.
24. When he cries out to God on the cross the people think he is invoking Elijah. They do not understand him.
25. Catholic relatives and friends often ask me questions that are answered very succinctly in several books that Our Sunday Visitor publishes: *Where Is That in the Bible?* by Patrick Madrid, and *The Catholic Answer Bible* with inserts by Paul Thigpen and Dave Armstrong are two good references.
26. Pope John Paul II, *Ecclesia de Eucharistia*, 22.
27. Ibid., *Mane Nobiscum Domine*, 19.
28. Ibid., 22.
29. Ibid., 28.
30. Ignatius of Antioch, *Letter to the Ephesians*, 20.
31. Pope John Paul II, *Mane Nobiscum Domine*, 24.
32. Ibid., 26.
33. Ibid., 26.
34. Ibid., 24.
35. Illustrations Unlimited, 361-62.
36. Pope John Paul II, *Ecclesia de Eucharistia*, 19-20.
37. Ibid., *Mane Nobiscum Domine*, 26.

ACKNOWLEDGMENTS

How to Get the Most Out of the Eucharist is the result of much thought and interaction with many people I have encountered along the way. While it is impossible to single out everyone responsible for the content of this book, I would like to mention a few.

First and foremost is Pope John Paul II, whose recent encyclical and apostolic letter on the Eucharist have sparked a movement within the Catholic Church that continues to fascinate me. The Pope is clearly steering all of us toward a renewed appreciation of the Eucharist and the role of Mary in helping us contemplate the face of Jesus ever more clearly.

Next is the late Orthodox Proto-presbyter Alexander Schmemann, whose work on the Eucharist I became acquainted with while writing *The How-To Book of the Mass*. Father Schmemann, who wrote from the Eastern Christian standpoint but with a Western sensibility, has given me a greater appreciation for the transcendent nature of the Eucharist and its impact on the way we live in the world while not being of the world.

Special thanks go to all of the following:

My home parish of St. John the Baptist in Fort Wayne, Indiana, and my pastor, Father Daryl Rybicki, for inviting me to speak on this topic at their yearly Spiritfest in 2002.

A number of people who raised questions when I first gave a talk on this subject at the national convention of the National Catholic Educators Association and the St. Louis Catechetical Conference in St. Louis in the spring of 2003.

The Daughters of St. Paul in Charleston, South Carolina, who sponsored a talk that I gave on this topic in 2003 at the Pauline Books and Media Center in Charleston and to all who attended the presentation and gave their excellent feedback; Bishop Robert Baker for inviting me to speak on the new mysteries of the Rosary at the Diocesan Rosary Rally in Lexington, South Carolina; Monsignor Joseph Roth, who presided at the daily Mass and the fine parish community that I mention in this book at the Cathedral of St. John the Baptist in Charleston that inspired me greatly.

Jennifer Shrader, who invited me to speak at St. Mary of the Assumption's Spiritfest in Van Wert, Ohio, in the fall of 2003. Those in attendance were the source of the question "Why do people care so little about their faith today?" mentioned on page 15.

Dave and Anita Eversole, owners of On a Wing and a Prayer in suburban Chicago, who were responsible for having Father Jerry Zalonis, M.I.C., invite me to do a parish mission in Plano, Illinois, in 2003. Father Jerry asked me a question at the end of the mission that haunted me for months and is one reason the Appendix was written. Bob and Lori Dressel and the staff at La Salle Manor Retreat Center gave me the peace and quiet I needed to reflect on all of these issues between mission talks.

Kurt Lucas, who invited me to speak on this topic as part of the Bishop Paul V. Donovan Lecture Series in Kalamazoo, Michigan, in 2004. His group of enthusiastic attendees gave me a full hour of questions to ponder.

My wife, Amy, and her many Open Book blog (amywelborn.typepad.com) readers who left comments at my Annunciations blog (michaeldubruiel.blogspot.com) and provided me with many issues they felt were keeping them from getting the most out of the Eucharist. Amy's own keen insights often raise the questions that I spend months attempting to answer.

Sandy Judd, for her hard work in editing this text — a writer is always humbled when his many errors are pointed out, and Sandy has done so with much charity; George Foster, who coordinated the editing in-house and whose dedication to both his work and faith is a constant source of inspiration to me.

Carol Elder Napoli, for using her God-given gifts to paint the inspiring image "Lifted Up" that graces the cover of this book (more info about Carol's painting is found on page 137); Tyler Ottinger, who designed a wonderful cover, and Laura Blost, who designed the interior of this book.

A word of thanks to some special friends who without knowing it have greatly affected my faith, especially when it comes to my participation at the Eucharist:

Father Joseph L. Cunningham, who, as a professor of liturgy, taught me much and laid the foundation for all that I have learned since.

Monsignor Vincent Haut and Father Terry Morgan, who in different ways taught me to question my own presuppositions, something that has served me well over the years.

Jeannie Richard and Nancy Madden, who have questioned me at times with questions that I hope they will find answered in this book.

Father Robert Wright, S.O.L.T., who many years ago inspired me when as a college student he asked the simple question one day at table: "Is this building up the body of Christ?" That question continues to ring in my ears twenty-five years later.

Pat and Virginia Harrington of All Saints Religious Goods in Fort Wayne, who always engage me in a lively discussion about whatever topic I may be currently writing about.

My good friends Anthony Fragapane, Brian Butterly, and Peter Morgan, who for many years have kept me focused on the relationship between our faith and its meaning to our lives.

Fathers Tom Guido, Brian Flanagan, and Robert Gibbons, who share their parish experiences to keep what I write "real" and applicable.

Finally, thanks to you the reader. May you find that this book helps you to draw closer to Christ and to experience his Kingdom ever more richly in your life.

ABOUT THE
COVER ART

The beautiful painting that graces the cover of this book, "Lifted Up," is a creation of Carol Elder Napoli, from New Smyrna Beach, Florida. I purchased it seven years ago at an exhibit of her work in Lakeland, Florida.

I remember commenting to Carol at the time that it would make the perfect image for the cover of a book that I intended to write someday. Thanks to the crafty cover design by Tyler Ottinger at Our Sunday Visitor, others can now enjoy this piece and meditate on its connection with the content of this book.

Of course, Carol had her own reason and inspiration for the work and I asked her to recall the origin of the piece:

> I remember this small work very well. It is my joy and passion to paint images that speak about the Lord, his love for us, and our life in him. Most often in my paintings I use the image of a lamb to represent our Savior, Jesus the Lamb of God. But one day I was praying with a friend who had stopped by my studio. She was going through a difficult time in her life, and we felt the need to stop talking with each other and talk to the Lord. After our time of prayer, my friend left and I closed my eyes to continue in prayer for a moment. In my mind's eye I saw the Lord as if he were on the cross, hanging with arms upraised. Between his arms and upon his back was a figure that I took to represent my troubled friend and all of us. We in our weakness and sin were the burden that I saw him car-

rying on that cross. The cup in the lower-right corner of the painting represents that cup that he took for each one of us. I am so grateful for his love and provision.

If you would like to see more of Carol's work, visit her website at www.napoliart.com.

TO CONTACT
THE AUTHOR

Michael Dubruiel has written seven personal growth and spirituality books, including the recently published *The Power of the Cross: Applying the Passion of Christ to Your Life*. He is a frequent speaker at Catholic events. To learn more, visit his website at www.michaeldubruiel.com. He can be contacted via e-mail at mdubruiel@osv.com or by writing to:

> Michael Dubruiel
> Our Sunday Visitor
> 200 Noll Plaza
> Huntington, IN 46750

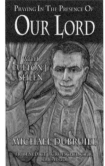

Our Sunday Visitor ...
Your Source for Discovering the Riches of the Catholic Faith

Our Sunday Visitor has an extensive line of materials for young children, teens, and adults. Our books, Bibles, pamphlets, CD-ROMs, audios, and videos are available in bookstores worldwide.

To receive a FREE full-line catalog or for more information, call **Our Sunday Visitor** at **1-800-348-2440, ext. 3**. Or write **Our Sunday Visitor** / 200 Noll Plaza / Huntington, IN 46750.

Please send me ____ A catalog
Please send me materials on:
____ Apologetics and catechetics
____ Prayer books
____ The family
____ Reference works
____ Heritage and the saints
____ The parish

Name _____

Address _____ Apt._____

City _____ State _____ Zip_____

Telephone ( ) _____

A53BBBBP

Please send a friend ____ A catalog
Please send a friend materials on:
____ Apologetics and catechetics
____ Prayer books
____ The family
____ Reference works
____ Heritage and the saints
____ The parish

Name _____

Address _____ Apt._____

City _____ State _____ Zip_____

Telephone ( ) _____

A53BBBBP

OurSundayVisitor

200 Noll Plaza, Huntington, IN 46750
Toll free: **1-800-348-2440**
Website: www.osv.com